Michael Hastings

THE CUTTING OF THE CLOTH

OBERON BOOKS
LONDON

WWW.OBERONBOOKS.COM

First published in 2015 by Oberon Books Ltd
521 Caledonian Road, London N7 9RH
Tel: +44 (0) 20 7607 3637 / Fax: +44 (0) 20 7607 3629
e-mail: info@oberonbooks.com
www.oberonbooks.com

A catalogue record for this book is available from the British
Library.

PB ISBN: 9781783198115
E ISBN: 9781783198160

Cover image by Jon Bradfield (from photos by Oksana Churakova
and Vitaly Korovin/Dreamstime)

Characters

SPIJAK WAZKI, *55*

MAURICE GARDNER, *16*

SYDIE WAZKI, *30*

ERIC, *50*

IRIS, *45*

and the RUNNER'S VOICE

ACT ONE

Scene One
A work-room of Kilgour. French & Stanbury,
a morning in September 1953.

Scene Two
An afternoon in December 1953.

ACT TWO

Scene One
A morning in June 1954.

Scene Two
An afternoon in December 1954.

ACT THREE

Scene One
A morning, 1st of January 1955.

Scene Two
A morning, 3rd of January 1955.

NOTE

A baste-job arrives on a maker's bench wrapped in brown paper and soft canvas.

All the pieces have been chalked and trimmed by the cutter in the front shop. This preliminary making-up is the baste for first fitting.

ACT ONE
SCENE ONE

The room is in a cellar. The windows are barred and give little light. Neon strips from the ceiling give a metallic colour. By the door to the street an internal phone hangs against the wall. The boards are bare.

There are three work benches. Each one is about eight feet in length. At the right end of each bench stands a couple of heavy goose-irons. One iron is wired to a current which is tied to the ceiling. The other – can be a wedge-shaped narrow dowsing iron or a beveller – is cordless. Each iron weighs 14lbs. Beside the irons there is a box for chalk, bodkins, threads and tapes. A foot above floor level, the length of each bench, there is a nod-step, it is filled with bundles, baste jobs, cloth rolls, slim sleeve boards and broader duplex boards for panel and seam pressing. On the opposite side of each bench stands a kipper's stool, her foot rest, and built in to the bench on her side are a number of drawers.

Side on to a wall stand two sewing machines; the foot plate is the old style pedal push. Pushed back against the side is a tall mirror on rollers. Brown paper patterns in clips hang on the walls. A radio perches on a shelf. A number of jackets in various states of finish hang on a steel clothes rail which can trolley up and down the room on the rollers.

Up a slight step from the floor level is part of a wall of tiles, and the side view of a lavatory cubicle is open.

SPIJAK is at his bench, opposite him works SYDIE on her stool. The bench, at a slight angle to his, is empty. ERIC is at his bench, and IRIS works a machine. The door opens and a RUNNER clatters down the stairs, calling out, as he throws the stringed paper bundles across the room on to the floor.

RUNNER'S VOICE: Eric!

ERIC retrieves it.

RUNNER'S VOICE: Eric!

Second bundle flies through the air.

SPIJAK: What about Spijak!

RUNNER'S VOICE: And Spijak!

SPIJAK catches the flying bundle. The door slams shut. ERIC holds up his two bundles.

ERIC: Are you busy, Spijak?

SPIJAK: Are you asking?

ERIC: I'm asking!

Triumphantly holding up both bundles. SPIJAK glares and brandishes his one bundle.

SPIJAK: Busy busy it isn't busy that makes a suit, it's work that does. You put my hands aside yours – sand and milk.

ERIC: But why do I get two jobs for every job come flying through the door for you – ?

SPIJAK: For why? Do I run to the machine? I'll sew the sideseam, I'll sew the shoulder, and I'll sew the facing – you and your machine don't cut no baste not with me – I can tell a machined jacket before it turns round the corner of the street.

ERIC: Iris and me have got speed.

SPIJAK: If you found a machine that went round in circles you'd machine tack every collar in the trade.

ERIC: This is the new world – there's technology –

SPIJAK: Is it true you machine linings – ?

ERIC: Well –

SPIJAK: I seen them in the street. There are hundreds of jackets with machine lined linings by Eric walking up and down Bond Street. And you don't care.

ERIC: I'm all the more grateful you should!

SPIJAK: It's lucky the needle was invented otherwise you'd stick everything through a mechanical slot machine and pow pow out it come like a pre-packed plastic wrapped British Railways' lettuce/tomato sandwich! And will you hand-stich a pocket flap –

ERIC: You won't dare look at my wage packet!

SPIJAK: You'd rather run a hot iron over your big toe than stitch out a pocket flap!

ERIC: Are you asking?

SPIJAK: I'm asking.

ERIC: I'm not listening.

SPIJAK: Course you get two jobs for every one of mine – You skimp the hand to feed the machine. Machine's the death of the hand. Now look at my hand – twenty to eight in the morning – and it's bleeding already!

SYDIE: He just cut himself with his own scissors –

SPIJAK: And I'll tell you one more thing I think about you Eric, I'll tell you –

IRIS looks up. She breaks the atmosphere in the room with a long sigh –

IRIS: It was such a lovely morning this morning, in the morning. I walked down to the pond and fed the pigeons.

SPIJAK stands with his mouth wide open in mid voice. ERIC stares at IRIS.

SPIJAK: What did she say?

ERIC: What do you want for to say a thing like that Iris – we were having a good time. Weren't we?

He looks across at SPIJAK. SPIJAK grins and thumps his sleevboard with the handblock. Thump thump thump!

SYDIE: *(Sewing.)* Pigeons were nice were they, Iris – ?

IRIS: Oh pigeons were wonderful…

SYDIE: Stand on your hand did they…

IRIS: Take the bread out of your finger nail they would.

SYDIE: Like a bit of breakfast come the cold…

IRIS: And they're so grateful.

ERIC: Old days were different.

SPIJAK: Time was when kippers kept their place and never spoke except to make the tea –

ERIC: My old boss's day – halfpenny out of wage packet every word said before twelve, or no end of bollocking.

SPIJAK: Pigeons!

ERIC: Old days were different –

SPIJAK: When I was first to learn the trade and the old makers started a quarrel about who made up best – how often they use the machine and like – blood would hit the ceiling.

ERIC: That's right.

SPIJAK: I'd hit you with the sleeve-board.

ERIC: I'd take the cap off the steam iron and give you a douse of hot boiling water over your tacked up tweed bridle. No end of shrink that'd do your customer!

SPIJAK: As it all was once wasn't it…

ERIC: As it all was…

SPIJAK: Now it's just pigeons…

SPIJAK works away. ERIC starts to open the bundles. SPIJAK tries to pretend not to look, but he cannot help it.

SPIJAK: … Eh Eric – what did you mean by saying I didn't dare look at your wage packet – ? Eric?

IRIS and SYDIE look up sharply.

ERIC: I meant what I meant. I meant –

SYDIE: How many pigeons did you say you can get on the palm of your hand, Iris?

IRIS: Oh I'll get six at a time – all peck peck peck and they nip little red nips in your skin if you don't put enough bread down too.

SPIJAK and ERIC shrug. SPIJAK bangs furiously with his handblock on shoulder pads. ERIC pulls out a rolled wad of cloth for making up, cut and chalked already, from the first bundle. IRIS leans over and touches the material.

ERIC: What's this, then – ?

IRIS: Tell him, Eric.

SPIJAK: He's not listening.

IRIS: Tell him what it is?

SPIJAK: *(To SYDIE.)* The guv'nor cuts out a two-piece thimble with inner face linings and Eric gets the paranoics!

SYDIE: Don't start a war – It's Tuesday morning.

SPIJAK: So it's Tuesday! He got what looked like a pair of shammy leather knee-caps on Monday, on Tuesday he's got a bespoke thimble to make up, what will he get on Wednesday? He'll get a sackweave tea-cosy and call it an Indian Rajah's polo jockstrap! What a mensh!

ERIC: Those knee-caps you referred to so rudely in passing –

SPIJAK: *(Waving shears.)* Clip clip clip – you'll cut your ears off Thursday and baste them down on the collar and call them a new style in fly-away!

ERIC: Those knee-caps were silk felt for a toff's hunt ball waistcoat –

IRIS: And we made them up in twenty minutes –

ERIC: And when was the last time you were represented by a good piece of cloth in a hunt ball!

SPIJAK attempts to open his own bundle. He sniffs it. He weighs it in his hands. He punches the paper wrapping. ERIC unfolds the jacket he has been sent to make up.

ERIC: *(With pleasure.)* Western Isles fine herring bone soft as a lily's lip – reckon that weight – reckon that weight Iris.

IRIS: Eight and a quarter ounces –

ERIC: Like jewelry that is!

SPIJAK: What you got to line it with – silver horsehair and gold thread!

ERIC: *(Pulling out the label.)* A Captain – Boyd Rochfort – a gent – Captain Boyd Rochfort – trains horses of the Queen –

He holds up the length of the back seam.

ERIC: Look at this – forty-six inches down his spine – and an eleven and a half inch shoulder that's what you call an aristocrat – all of six and a half feet tall and built like a guardsman! That's style for you, Spijak.

SPIJAK: Now he's in the Queen's box at Newmarket rubbing up with the royals!

ERIC: Remember that black tails with the purple linings last year – what did that get me –

SPIJAK: Ought to have got you three years the amount of machining you did to it.

ERIC: Paddock enclosure ticket for nothing, and I went up to the tails and I watched them.

SPIJAK: What do you mean you watched?

SYDIE: Watched the horses!

ERIC: – I was watching my tails!

IRIS: Was he nice to them?

ERIC: Nice! What does a bloke like that – money in his ears – care about his tails. Nice! Dropped two bloody marys and a dollop of beef burger ketchup down his facings didn't he?!

ERIC holds up a pair of leather elbow patches.

SPIJAK: What's that?

ERIC: *(Handling them to IRIS.)* Some clever trick for his Newmarket racing.

SYDIE: Couple of elbow patches!

SPIJAK: What did you think they were Eric – pair of blinkers for you to see by when you're on the machine!

ERIC: I understand the likes of Capatin Rochfort – they're not mugs – riding a horse up and down the paddocks every morning – got to keep the rough off the old elbows.

SPIJAK: I ain't never heard of a geezer going to the most expensive bespoke shop in London – and ordering himself a pair of elbow patches. Have you Sydie?

SYDIE: Never, Dad.

SPIJAK: He must have come in the front shop – Captain Whatnot – and said who's making up this load of old rubbish? Eric they say. Eric! What Eric Machine Mad Eric down in the cellars! I need a bit of protection. Chuck in the elbow blinkers, that Eric's a butcher!

ERIC opens another bundle. It is a shiny job for make up.

ERIC: Black silk alpaca with a rough finish surface.

IRIS: *(Reading the label.)* Mr. Bernard Delfont!

SPIJAK: Never heard of him.

ERIC: Show business. Big impresario.

SPIJAK: In the history of tailoring you learn one thing – Dukes, Earls and Impresarios never pay their bills. You can forget about that one! That'll never see the light of day on Albemarle Street.

ERIC: Now he's an expert on impresarios and the history of bespoke!

IRIS holds up the instruction slip.

IRIS: Important to take note: damp press thoroughly and tuft out both sleeve heads, and empty shoulder pads to half.

ERIC: Shoulders pads to half …

SPIJAK: Means he don't want to be seen down Wardour Street with a spiv's pair of shoulders or a suit what lights up like the Aurora Borealis – that's what.

ERIC: That's dignified isn't it? No use turning up at a cocktail party in the Bahamas with Noël Coward and Mr. and Mrs. Jack Heinz looking like a strip joint promoter down Berwick Market.

SPIJAK: So now he's at a cocktail party on the prom pier in the Bahamas with American millionaires.

ERIC: I can see this jacket – sitting in the evening sun – watching the yacht out there on the briny blue – there's a full piece orchestra in white Aquascutum tuxedos and this butler's coming over the marble floor with daiquiri bitters and twists of lemon!

SPIJAK: How's it going Duchess, I'm Eric the impresario what's yours to be? Half a pint shandy in your no-cup bra and I'll see you on the beach in ten minutes!

SYDIE opens SPIJAK's bundle. SPIJAK takes the pieces out.

SPIJAK: Serge…

SYDIE: Apple moss lining…

SPIJAK: Why do they always send me the slant and flap pocket jobs, when – if there is one job which can hold up proper making – it's these.

ERIC: They must like your fingers, mate.

SYDIE: *(Taking out the instructions.)* Pay close attention to irregularities.

SPIJAK: Irregularities?

ERIC: It's a camel's dressing gown!

SPIJAK takes out the separate pieces and measures some seams with a tape.

SPIJAK: Twenty-seven inch left arm, nineteen inch right arm. Seven inches left shoulder, nine and a quarter inches the right.

He picks up the instruction note.

SPIJAK: Stretch out the left shoulder blade on board head, thin out left shoulder back padding, and allow a loose stitch at top of back seam for give.

ERIC: It's a camel's hump!

SPIJAK: *(Reading.)* Make turn-up cuffs and remember to shrink the back cellar under felt. I've got turn back cuffs, a hump like Silbury Hill, one arm a foot shorter than the other and flap pocket jobs up and down his front like a patchwork quilt! It's a cripple!

ERIC: Got to hand it to you guv'nor – when he's got a right cripple he knows which bench to send it to! Now that's a compliment to your uncanny ability to hand-make miracles.

SPIJAK: Eric! Do you want us to come to blows?

ERIC: Are you threatening?

SPIJAK: I'm threatening!

SYDIE looks nervously across at IRIS.

SYDIE: Would you like us both to buy a loaf of bread, Iris, take it in the park at lunch time – feed the pigeons?

IRIS: That would be nice wouldn't it. Bit of fresh air –

ERIC hammers his cloth on the ham.

ERIC: *(Disarmingly.)* I love you Spijak – you can threaten all morning if you like – love you.

SPIJAK smiles and snares his thread, and snaps it off to lace up the needle again.

SPIJAK: *(To the girls.)* … Pigeons! …

They are working quietly. IRIS uses a sewing machine, which makes a heavy rattle of a noise.

The door opens. MAURICE steps in. He takes off his overcoat and stands waiting for SPIJAK to turn around.

SYDIE: *(Nudging SPIJAK.)* … Spijak…

SPIJAK: I know.

SYDIE: Speak to him –

SPIJAK: He's the boy isn't he?

SYDIE: Please –

SPIJAK: *(Without looking around.)* You're late!

MAURICE: Excuse me –

SPIJAK: Sir –

MAURICE: Sir –

SPIJAK: You're late boy.

SYDIE: It's not eight o'clock yet, how can he be late?

MAURICE: It's ten to eight.

SPIJAK: So? In ten minutes it'll be eight o'clock, then tomorrow you'll turn up and it'll be just on eight o'clock; the day after you'll be here at ten past eight! In a week's time you'll be waltzing in here at half past ten!

SYDIE: It's his second day in the trade and you're terrifying him.

SPIJAK: I ask myself is that unreasonable? To be terrified in your second day at work? I think what it was like when I started on the bench – I was so terrified of my boss every time he spoke I came out in a sweat like a Hong Kong flu virus! You can take it from me boy – You'll be in a state of terror long after the day you can tell the difference between a collar canvas and a boomerang.

MAURICE: What time must I be here then – ?

SPIJAK: I want you in the door twenty-five minutes before it's time for you to be late!

MAURICE: Yes, sir.

SPIJAK: Get on the bench, boy!

MAURICE takes off his jacket, and climbs up on the empty bench. He tries to cross his legs. He finds it difficult.

SPIJAK: Are you sitting as you should be sitting?

MAURICE: Yes –

SPIJAK: You're not sitting at all.

He places a long board across the boy's knees to flatten them down. He places the boy's elbows on each knee and presses them down. It hurts.

SPIJAK: And push down with your elbows. Push the knee down until they ache.

MAURICE: They do.

MAURICE shakes his head. He takes a revers already tacked on to a front panel of cloth and renews padding it in long rolled stiches where he left off the night before. A silver thimble appears on his right fore-finger. He works with his right hand with obvious difficulty.

SPIJAK glowers at the boy, and walks all around the bench tutting and sniffing until the boy has to look up.

MAURICE: … Am I doing something wrong – ?

SYDIE: Maurice…

She gently leans forward.

SYDIE: … Real makers don't ever use thimbles.

MAURICE: I brought it because…

SPIJAK: You ain't a woman are you – ?

MAURICE: It hurts without it sir –

SPIJAK: Of course it does. How else do you learn you're stitching it right without it hurting you?

SYDIE: His finger was bleeding yesterday.

SPIJAK: If it doesn't bleed how else does he learn how not to make it bleed? Right – Eric?

ERIC: Right.

SPIJAK: The nail on your forefinger must look like the face of the moon before you work your first month.

ERIC: Then it swells up –

SPIJAK: And when it swells down you can't feel it it's so numb.

ERIC: And when you can't feel it – you can't tell the difference between working a brick wall and a piece of cotton wool.

SPIJAK takes a hand-wriiten sheet out of the wooden box on the top of his bench.

SPIJAK: What's this boy?

MAURICE: My contract, sir.

SPIJAK: What does it say if you piss off?

MAURICE: Null and void sir.

SPIJAK: And will I give you any recommendation for another job? No sir, I won't sir.

SPIJAK takes a pin and tacks the contract on to the wall.

SPIJAK: Maurice Gardner, aged sixteen, hereby declares he will work a four and a half year apprenticeship under the said Spijak Wazki, at a basic rate of twenty-eight shilling a week, in order that he may qualify in bespoke and garment making as a first-class tailor or thereabouts. Signed Maurice, hereinafter always referred to as the apprentice; signed Spijak, hereinafter always referred to as the master craftsman, and more commonly known as 'sir' or 'that bleeding tyrant' according to the amount of fear and pain your earthly body is the begetter of!

MAURICE: *(Lowers his head and sews.)* Yes sir.

SPIJAK draws a breath. He studies the boy.

IRIS: … Shame!

ERIC: Day I first sat on the bench my guv'nor had me knees tied to the underside with stay tape. And wouldn't undo them until my knees were level with my ankles.

SYDIE: If I was a boy, Iris, I wouldn't come into this trade – would you?

IRIS: Course not.

SYDIE: Roomful of foul-mouthed makers –

IRIS: Never give a lad a chance.

SPIJAK studies the boy's sewing. MAURICE tries but he can't get it right. His fingers fumble.

SPIJAK: … Show us it, boy.

MAURICE holds it up. All the padding stitches which should roll the revers with vertical strokes have gone very awry. SPIJAK holds it up. ERIC has to smile at it.

SPIJAK: I won't make a comment. I won't say a word. I'll show it to Eric. What's this Eric? Is this sewing or is it some kind of new-fangled knitting?

ERIC takes the revers and holds it to the light.

ERIC: It's a sort of petit point.

SPIJAK snatches the revers back.

SPIJAK: It's a sort of something, but it's not sort of padding stitch. How many times yesterday did I teach you to pad the canvas over your fingers until it rolled? You just nick the cloth under-side – you don't leave such a thread underside as wide as a washing line!

MAURICE: Please sir –

SPIJAK: No sir –

SYDIE: Let him say!

MAURICE: I'm left-handed sir!

SPIJAK pauses. The news sinks in. SYDIE has to laugh quietly.

IRIS: … Oh, it's a shame.

SPIJAK: I thought the last boy I had was bright. He did two year on his apprenticeship and somehow, after I had nearly killed him for twenty-four months, he persuaded the army he was fit enough to join National Service and go to Malaya. But beside him, you're a genius! You collect the biggest prize of them all! Two days at the trade, and you announce you are so handicapped you can't even work with your right hand! What are you doing to me! Why do you think the scissors are moulded to a right-hand grip? Why do you think the dolly lives on the right-hand side? Why did Almighty God and the brains of Kilgour, French and Stanbury design benches with the irons on the right-hand side!

MAURICE: I'm afraid I've always been like that –

SPIJAK: Before we progress to the third day of your apprenticeship – God willing you ever see the light of such a day – just what else is the matter with you – ?

MAURICE: Nothing so far as I –

SPIJAK: You're next going to tell me you're not a Jew at all –

MAURICE: Well, my Father was a German Jew – but he was brought up in Wales –

SPIJAK: That's right. I know. Your Mother's got goyisher kop and you couldn't get an Israeli passport if you married the fourteenth yid of a fourteenth yid.

MAURICE: Sir, my Mother was Dutch but she was born in the Potteries.

IRIS: You tell him lad.

MAURICE: Before the war, my Father was the best cutter in Regent Street.

SPIJAK: When I count the bespoke shops in that street on the back of a needle, he must have been the only cutter in the whole of Regent Street. When was your Bar Mitzvah?

MAURICE: It wasn't possible because –

SPIJAK: Course it wasn't. What happened? On his way there, the Rabbi fell down a manhole and read the six hundred and thirteen Commandments to the five-thirty rush hour at Clapham Junction underground. Course it wasn't possible. And were you even circumcised – ?

SYDIE: If there's one thing my Dad likes to talk about it's somebody else's circumcision.

IRIS: Oh, it's a shame.

MAURICE: As a matter of fact –

SPIJAK: Should I be so vulgar to ask!

IRIS: I wouldn't tell my boss if I was circumcised or not. Would you Sydie – ?

SYDIE: Course not.

SPIJAK: What happened? I can see it now – a V2 bomb made a direct hit on the hospital the instant the Rabbi raised up his knife!

SPIJAK holds up the bundle of serge with the special measurements.

SPIJAK: Eric says this is a cripple! I'm the only master craftsman mug in Dover Street who's found himself a Welsh-born German Dutch Potter apprentice who never took his Bar Mitzvah, who was never circumcised, and who can just stitch a baste seam with his big left toe. With such a boy for an apprentice who needs a wage packet!

The telephone against the wall by the door starts to ring. It has a strident internal bell. ERIC races for the phone.

IRIS: Sydie…go on…give him a hand.

As SPIJAK works on his bench, SYDIE stands by MAURICE to help him.

ERIC: Yes guv'nor?

SYDIE: … You see – you'll just have to work with your right hand, Maurice. You'll have to learn like this…

ERIC: *(Into the phone.)* … No guv'nor. Well what would I do? How do I know what I'd do! I'm not there am I? … What would I most like in life? I'd like a three-piece vicuna with matching overcoat and gameskeeper's cap. You can't find the client? Don't bother. I'll make it up anyway – and I'll take it Isow's Restaurant and I'll strip the first mogul I see.

ERIC hangs the phone back on its hook. He retruns to his bench.

ERIC: … That was the guv'nor, that was.

SPIJAK: Hardly likely it was a baste-neck canvas collar and a remould sleeve-head talking down the phone.

ERIC: Talking to me.

SPIJAK: So you've got a friend in high places.

ERIC: Asking for my advice.

SPIJAK: Now we got a new firm of guv'nors – now we got Kilgour, French, Stanbury and Eric.

ERIC: 'Is that you Eric? Can you manage two more double-breasted worsteds Eric? No Sir I'm up to my ears in hair-cloth.'

SYDIE: About all he's got between his –

ERIC: The guv'nor's racing up and down the front shop like a headless chicken. Eric, he says, I got those two property men in the cubicles. One's Mr. Clore, and other's Mr. Fenston, and he says, he's darting in and out of either cubicle listening to them – and they both think they've bought the same piece of property. What shall he do, the guv'nor asks me? Me!

IRIS: Eric always wanted to be a cutter in the front shop.

ERIC: I'd have strolled from one to the other – cool as crepe silk – take it easy Mr. Clore keep your flap-pocket bar tacks open just in case of Mr. Fenston. Hold on to your selvedge trims Mr. Fenson you don't want your threads running loose when Mr. Clore's got his scissors out.

IRIS: I always said Eric would make a nifty front shop man. Eric's got the lingo.

ERIC: The first rule of a front shop cutter is never to wear a better suit than what the customer has got on.

SPIJAK: Well with your machine artistry at making up you wouldn't have much trouble on that score, would you?

ERIC: But he rang me up didn't he?

IRIS: Course he did. He likes Eric.

ERIC: He didn't ring Spijak up did he?

IRIS: Eric's got style.

MAURICE: That may be – but I reckon my boss has got craft.

SPIJAK: *(To MAURICE.)* Just you belt up and don't show your stitches underside, boy. Me and Eric were having a converse –

MAURICE: I was only standing up for –

SPIJAK: When I need you to stand up for me I'll turn over to Eric a month in wage packets!

SPIJAK takes the jacket he has been working, and puts it on.

SPIJAK: Now boy…you may not hear our friend Eric tell you this – but I want you to know there is one rule only about good clothes. And that's what makes it an art – and that's a word what won't pass Eric's lips too quickly. Right Eric?

He shows ERIC the collar.

SPIJAK: Go on touch it Eric. Don't be afraid of it. Short on his throat he is and thick on his neck.

ERIC shakes the collar and taps it into place.

SPIJAK: You couldn't do that you butcher you…

He turns back to MAURICE

SPIJAK: The art is – this geezer's walking down the street and you're walking up to him. And you just can't stop staring at him? Why's that?

MAURICE: It's because –

SPIJAK: Because he's under-dressed, that's why you're looking at him. You walk and you're looking at him. You walk past him, this time, without looking at his front, you walk past him you turn around and stare at him. Why do you turn around and stare at him?

MAURICE: I'm turning around to stare at him because –

SPIJAK: You ain't you ain't. You're turning around to stare at him because over-dressed that's what.

MAURICE: I'm sorry I –

SPIJAK: The art of a perfectly made good suit is that –

SPIJAK holds out the book flaps for ERIC to see.

SPIJAK: Go on ask me if there's one machine stitch in them flaps? You don't dare you don't. That's my hands Eric – my hands in every flap there that is.

SPIJAK approaches MAURICE.

SPIJAK: Art of a perfectly made suit is that you don't notice it at all because it's so well made, it fits so natural, there's no cause to ask yourself if this twit is badly dressed or not. When a good suit is a good piece of making it's so good it's invisible. And that's craft, boy.

As SPIJAK takes the jacket off, ERIC takes two jackets over to the machine. He sits at the machine to run up.

SPIJAK: … And there's Eric doing his bit for progress there – he'd rather run his Grandmother's coffin under the machine than let the undertaker hammer and nail it. Eric's such a progressive.

MAURICE: Yes Sir.

ERIC machines pieces of two jackets. IRIS has her head down. SYDIE works away. SPIJAK walks around the boy's bench. He studies the boy's work.

SPIJAK: … And what are you feeling boy?

MAURICE: Bloody terrified, sir.

SPIJAK: I should say. And what are your fingers doing, boy?

MAURICE: Trembling, sir.

SPIJAK: And what is your honest opinion of me, boy?

MAURICE: I reckon you're a bleeding tyrant, Sir.

SPIJAK: And what are you going to do when that back end of that needle goes through your nail?

MAURICE: Let it bleed, sir, I'm going to let it bleed.

SPIJAK: And even if I kill you doing it what am I going to turn you into?

MAURICE: I don't know – I suppose –

ERIC machines pieces of two jackets.

SYDIE: He's going to make you into another bleeding tyrant bespoke craftsman.

IRIS: Oh… It's a shame!

MAURICE holds up his hand.

MAURICE: Sir…my finger is already bleeding.

SPIJAK: Don't ever let it stop.

SPIJAK goes back to his bench. ERIC finishes his machine work, takes the machined pieces to the bench. MAURICE tries hard to work on.

SYDIE: *(To IRIS.)* You got a backyard ain't you Iris?

IRIS: Ever so small.

SYDIE: But that's a privy shed out back isn't it?

IRIS: Catch me using it.

SYDIE: What I mean is – have you ever thought of pigeons?

IRIS: I haven't when you mention it like –

SYDIE: Keep quite a few there you could –

IRIS: Well I'll remember that.

SYDIE: White ones make a wonderful sound.

IRIS: I'll ask… I'll ask the neighbour.

ERIC bangs his sleeveblock on the ham. SPIJAK bangs his on the table as loudly as they can to drown the pigeon subject.

A jangling bell announces one o'clock. ERIC and SPIJAK down tools immediately. They reach for their coats. They both wear hats.

ERIC: Lunch already Spijak.

SPIJAK: Pub already.

They make for the door.

SPIJAK: *(To MAURICE.)* You be here boy – you're running this afternoon boy – you're running to the front shop and back for fittings with every baste job I can remember I've ever made.

ERIC: Iris – I want all the cotton reels counted and marked up for the chits by when I get back.

Both men head for the door as rapidly as they can. IRIS shrugs. She collects her bag and her scarf. The men clatter up the front steps to the street. IRIS follows them.

IRIS: ...secretaries don't get treated like this no more. We need a union we do.

SYDIE is about to follow IRIS. She turns back. MAURICE is having great difficulty with his knees on the bench.

SYDIE: Ain't you got nowhere to go then – ?

MAURICE: It's my knees!

SYDIE: Dad only allows boys forty-five minutes.

MAURICE: I can't move. It's my knees. I'm paralysed! Sydie!

SYDIE grins and runs out.

It is dark for a few moments. When the lights lift the workroom is empty. The bathroom downstairs is in darkness. Then SYDIE returns from her lunch hour with a packet of sandwiches. She takes off her coat.

SYDIE: ... Maurice – ?

The light lifts in the bathroom. MAURICE is sat on the down-turned seat of the lavatory bowl. He is fully dressed but he appears to be choking. The door of the cubicle is open.

SYDIE runs down the steps into the bathroom. She sees the boy sitting there.

SYDIE: … I knew you weren't going out for lunch.

MAURICE: You did – ?

He doesn't seem to care any whether she did or not. He looks very pale.

SYDIE: I knew you hadn't any money – didn't I – ?

MAURICE: I've got bus fare.

She holds out the sandwiches towards him.

SYDIE: So I got you egg and tomato and salmon and cucumber.

At that instant, MAURICE chokes, doubles ever, then turns around and leans over the lavatory bowl to vomit up. His stomach heaves.

SYDIE: … Hang about – you haven't tasted them yet!

MAURICE: *(Sicking up.)* Glass of water…!

She pours water from the basin tap into a mug. MAURICE takes the water. Sits back on the lavatory crown and drinks. SYDIE pulls the chain. The cistern flushes.

SYDIE: … Anyway…what are you doing sitting in this place for?

MAURICE: I especially like to be in here don't I – ?

SYDIE: Well what you doing being sick then?

MAURICE: Shutup shutup on me!

SYDIE leans against the wash stand. She watches him. How he covers his face with his hands, and she knows he had no intention of shouting like that.

SYDIE: … It's not always like this…

MAURICE: Course it is…

SYDIE: Comes a later time – and suddenly you can. Then you can shout.

MAURICE: I'm not here to study shouting. I'm here to study making up aren't I?

SYDIE: It gets better.

MAURICE: I had a schoolmaster in Chemistry who once set light to my hair – he said that too – it'll get better he said. I'm not here to get better. I'm not in an asylum.

SYDIE: The last boy – Mickey – when he started with Spijak he had a nervous breakdown and developed a twitch in his right eye.

MAURICE: So he was lucky – I'm just going to commit suicide, that's all!

SYDIE: Oddly enough – when Mickey developed that twitch in his eye he began to drop one bar-tack in every four when he sewed. Nobody noticed the twitch until Spijak lost his knot over the stitching.

MAURICE: What are you trying to tell me – ?

SYDIE: All the apprentices get hell eaten out of them until they can stand up to the guv'nor.

MAURICE: I'll kill him before I have to stand up to him!

SYDIE: He took me out of school at fourteen to be his kipper.

MAURICE: That ain't even legal –

SYDIE: My mother was ill – and she'd worked the bench for him as his kipper until–

MAURICE: But you still don't have to leave school at fourteen to –

SYDIE: I had to.

MAURICE: No you never.

SYDIE: She died.

MAURICE looks up at her. SYDIE balances the packet of sandwiches in her hands. She throws the sandwiches for him to catch.

SYDIE: … If you don't like these I can run across and change them –

MAURICE: Thanks. What do I owe you?

SYDIE: Nothing.

MAURICE: But I'm not going to be able to pay you back –

SYDIE: That's all right.

MAURICE: … You're very kind, then.

SYDIE goes to the door of the bathroom. As if to leave.

MAURICE: … You never said – what your Mother died of –

SYDIE: I wasn't going to.

MAURICE: Well she didn't just die like drop dead did she – ?

SYDIE: She died that's all.

MAURICE: Don't bother to tell me will you – ?

SYDIE: There's only one seam he'll run up on a machine – there's the back seam and that's how he's made up all his life. And did his Father the same. And before him. And before before.

MAURICE: So – ?

SYDIE: My Mother did everything Spijak ever told her. She did it all her life. And she still did nothing right. The day she died he was still shouting at her. He was shouting in the Service and he was still shouting when they burned her.

SYDIE shuts the door and hurries up the steps to the workroom.

She sits behind the bench and picks up her work. There are tears but we don't hear them.

The boy starts after her as if to call to her. He stops. He turns around and kicks the packet of sandwiches across the floor. He steps inside the cubicle and slams the door shut. He firmly locks it He sits there, very still and detached.

The lights lower.

SCENE TWO

It is in the afternoon, in December 1953, three months on. It is five o'clock. ERIC and MAURICE work on their benches. Behind the benches sit SYDIE and IRIS. On the nod-step beneath his bench SPIJAK is asleep. Occasionally he snores. The room is darker. There are different suits in various stages of make-up on the rolley.

ERIC: … What you working, son – ?

SYDIE: Making a waistcoat.

ERIC: Catch you he will – wake up and catch you and there'll be none of me own.

SYDIE: He won't wake.

MAURICE: Don't rightly care if he does.

IRIS: … Cocky now…

ERIC: Three months on the bench and he'll be asking for his guv'nor's wage packet

IRIS: How far has he learned you Maurice?

MAURICE: Never you mind, Iris.

ERIC: Three months on the bench and he's carving up kippers with his tongue. When I was a boy –

MAURICE: Eric when you was a boy the bobbin hadn't been invented.

ERIC: I was sworn to silence for the first year, and I was allowed to make tea the second – and on the third I was the runner from Hackney town hall steps to Park Lane.

One tram fare I was allowed – if it was wet – to run back
the baste-ups. Half moon steels and toe tacks under me
boots and I moved I did.

IRIS: You was a wonderful runner weren't you Eric?

ERIC: On the fourth year I was faster with the thread than any
kipper and only then did I get to the making up.

IRIS: When Eric and me get a rush-job I've seen Eric tack and
fell twice my speed. Eric's a very fast tack and fell man –

SYDIE: Eric don't tack and fell now Iris you just –

MAURICE: Eric don't tack and fell Eric takes it on the machine
and hammer and nails it. Don't you Eric?

ERIC: Lip from a lad like you –

IRIS: One thing your guv'nor never tells you is manners.

MAURICE: But perhaps he's right.

ERIC: Perhaps! When the front room boss rings down does
he ring for Spijak? Have I ever asked you that? Does he?
Course he don't.

SYDIE: He always knows we're busy –

ERIC: Knows you got two jobs to do this week and it's a cross
eyed likely miracle they be done the day the client walks
in front!

SYDIE: But we're craft Eric!

ERIC: If he was awake I'd tell him he's craft – yes he's craft –
he's crafting bloody stupid!

IRIS: Eric and me finish four in a week and baste two for first
fittings and have them semi-finished on the rolley before –

MAURICE: That's right Iris. You and Eric is a kind of all
purpose Montague Burton doubles act. Sunday night at
the London Palladium – the fastest bespoke machinists
in London! Frankie Laine orders the suit. Does his first

number – steps up on the stage at the end and there's Eric – pedalling his machine like a go-kart and before the curtain comes down Frankie Laine's taking his bow in his new jacket! What a bodge!

SYDIE: What a bodge!

MAURICE: Introducing – care of Kilgour, French and Stanbury – Montague and Burton! The flying tailors!

SPIJAK stirs. He snores; then he snorts into near waking.

ERIC: Lo the sleeper rises.

SYDIE: Let him be.

ERIC: Won't do such talking boy – the moment when.

MAURICE: See if I don't.

ERIC: Take it to Ladbroke's I will you won't.

ERIC takes a seam job to the machine and runs it up.

SYDIE: … What did you think Maurice – when you started what did you think it would be like?

MAURICE: It couldn't have been worse – what I thought

SYDIE: Spijak will never say so – he was proud you lasted that first week.

MAURICE: Well I weren't no Mickey was I? I had no nervous breakdown.

SYDIE: But what did your school friends think?

MAURICE: They had cushy jobs. Eight pound fifteen for a five day – they was insurance clerks – and they got BSA 250's down Coldharbour Lane and they can afford a girl go out on a Saturday and a Sunday.

SYDIE: There's that Locarno in Brixton Hill –

MAURICE: Well I can't dance can I? So there isn't much cop
in sorting out half my wages to look a right baste job doing
the tango.

SYDIE: But there's a nice girl somewhere.

MAURICE: Believe you me – on twenty-eight bob a week
there's not a nice girl within five quid of that.

ERIC: … Tell this sleeping princess it's five o'clock and
he's been missing more crooked seams than I can sew
blindfold.

SYDIE: What would you rather have – my Father out of the
pub and talking or out of the pub and taking his rest – ?

IRIS: Best thing an old soak like that learnt was to turn in on it –

ERIC: Wonder you ever got – you and your Father – ever got
any money to get back to Billericay on a night.

IRIS: Amount Spijak drinks.

ERIC: Did you ever think lad – you'd meet a maker what
pours so much down his front panels midday he can't
stand until he sleeps it off??

*SPIJAK shakes his head and looks up. He grunts – he sits up, bangs
his head on the lower side of the bench, and lies back prone again.*

SPIJAK: … What's this?

ERIC: Don't worry Spijak – it ain't your coffin.

*MAURICE hurriedly hides his waistcoat under another jacket on his
bench. He reaches for a jacket front.*

SPIJAK: … Where was I – ?

ERIC: Crown and Anchor you was – and you just about
managed to canvas and fell your way across D'Arblay
Street you did.

SPIJAK: Where's that boy?

ERIC: Doing better than you think – he's just bar tacked those vicuna sleeve heads and done a damp cloth shrink on the shoulder seams there he has.

SPIJAK: Where was I?

MAURICE: In the middle of my orals –

SPIJAK: You're looking at Mr. Stanbury's special cut up for a new customer. He wants to impress the customer. So he puts some irregular marks with the chalk on the tacking edges. He puts a slant slant slant shape on the edge, and what do you think?

MAURICE: Don't shrink it when sewn just –

SPIJAK: You stretch it.

ERIC: Nine out of ten.

SPIJAK: And there is another irregular chalk up – this time it's a series of wiggle lines.

MAURICE: Don't stretch it under the machine or by hand – shrink it in as –

SPIJAK: As best as you see fit.

ERIC: Ten out of ten.

IRIS: Very good.

MAURICE: Was I right this time?

SPIJAK: When I say you're right you're single wrong!
When I say you're wrong you're double wrong!

IRIS: … Shame.

SPIJAK: Where's your collar?

MAURICE: Around my neck, sir.

ERIC: Can't argue with that can you – !

SPIJAK: It's your new jacket. You're the customer. You stand up and the collar stands away as if it doesn't belong to you at all. You say – hallo that's queer. It's not a fly-away buttondown it's a fly-away collar on a three piece serge what is going to put me back ninety guineas.

MAURICE: I take it to the maker. I say – look at this bodge Eric I say – you been at the machine too much again –

IRIS: Shame to take the piss out of my Eric.

SPIJAK: Eric says he don't know what to do with that why don't you do a few barbell exercises and thicken up your neck to fit my collar!

MAURICE: The remedy is to let out the inlays at the gorge, reduce the width of the shoulder at scye point the corresponding amount; to ascertain –

IRIS: Never heard of that word have you Sydie – ?

MAURICE: To ascertain the exact measure rip all the shoulder, seam, neck, and front scye, and pass the material backwards thus decreasing the circumference of the stand-away.

SYDIE: Good on you Maurice!

MAURICE draws a deep breath and watches SPIJAK climb up from underneath his bench.

IRIS: Tell him it ain't true, Eric.

ERIC: Course it ain't true.

ERIC is trying on a completed jacket. It is a soft tweed sporting jacket. SPIJAK has a feel of it.

SPIJAK: No hard feelings Eric…

ERIC: No hard feelings…

SPIJAK: What's this load of old rubbish then.

ERIC: Ten and a half ounces herringbone. Best Lincoln wool and tweed together. Soft as a baby's bum.

SPIJAK: Who's it for – the Queen of Tonga?

ERIC: Mr. Harold Macmillan. When did you last do a Harold Macmillan?

SPIJAK: Never heard of him.

ERIC: Minister of Housing that's who. Don't get any jacked up property millionaires in this corner Spijak. Don't get any spare part tycoons here flogging off old car batteries.

ERIC saunters around in the jacket. Puffs himself up in it and brushes down the lapels.

I'm standing inside a bloke what built three hundred thousand houses this year –

SPIJAK: Bit of Jerry building in those shoulders isn't there – ?

ERIC: Sloping shoulders these. I know the Macmillan family very well. All got the same problem. Narrow shoulders with a definite slope. Too much hard work at cabinet official papers. Too much leaning over –

IRIS: Tell him where he's going in that jacket?

ERIC: Stands to reason don't it?

SPIJAK: Where's he going – the bog?

ERIC: Bloody not going to the bog mate – going to the moors he is isn't he, Iris?

IRIS: Stands to reason.

SPIJAK: Moors?

ERIC: Going to the moors up in Scotland – with his titled mates – and stalking the grouse he is in this.

ERIC takes an imaginary gun and fires off a couple of rounds. ERIC ducks behind a bench –

Flap flap flap – there they go –

ERIC leaps up from behind the bench firing off –

Bang bang! Two in the bag for tomorrow's lunch that was! There's the dogs belting down the dingle –

SPIJAK: Dingle what dingle?

ERIC: Yappety yap – here boy – here boy – says the gillie –

SPIJAK: What's a gillie?

ERIC: Trouble with you Spijak is you ain't got the feel of the client. This jacket's going to hide behind bushes –

SPIJAK: I'm not surprised when I look at it –

ERIC: And out it comes with a twelve bore gun knocking them grouse out of the sky like a fairground coco-nut shy!

SPIJAK: So I should be impressed!

IRIS: Eric's got a very good imagination. Eric has.

ERIC: When Mr. Macmillan sees a couple of grouse lying around – and nobody's watching – he'll thank me when he slips a couple of them in his pockets and whips them home to the wife on the quiet – thank me he will for giving his pockets a double width lining!

SPIJAK: I thought you said he was the Minister of Housing?

ERIC: So I did.

SPIJAK: The way you done his pockets – you'd think he was Jack Rabbit and his dog, the midnight thieving poacher!

MAURICE: … What do I do with this now – ?

SPIJAK: All those side seams handstitched – ?

MAURICE: Both sides.

SPIJAK: Not like Eric and his machine work – ?

MAURICE: Right.

SPIJAK: So now it's the back seam and that's the only seam you'll see me put under the bobbin.

SPIJAK turns back to the bench. MAURICE takes the seam and presses it on the ironing cloth on the bench.

IRIS: I reckon it's half past five now, Sydie – don't you – ?

SYDIE: I never keep my watch slow.

IRIS: Nor do I…

SPIJAK: My boss and his kipper stay all the evening and he had her making his supper right here on the bench he did.

ERIC: That's right – no kippers skiving off.

IRIS and SYDIE at a glance – get up and take their aprons off. IRIS reaches for her hat and coat. SYDIE slings her coat over her arm.

SYDIE: … T'rra lads…

IRIS: *(Taking her by the arm.)* Nice port and lemon Sydie…

SYDIE: Glad to get away.

They walk out together. As they go both SPIJAK and ERIC kick up a terrific noise with their hand blocks. They continue until the girls have closed the door behind them and their footsteps have passed up the stone steps to the street outside.

SPIJAK lifts off his press board a finished jacket. It is made of a tough brown serge. SPIJAK with a certain amount of pride holds up the coat with his fist in the shoulder to test it for balance. He tries the other shoulder. He swings it about to put air through the sleeve.

SPIJAK: … Take a gander at that…

ERIC: Took you nigh all of ten days to finish off that.

SPIJAK: I suppose you could have run it up in your lunch hour –

ERIC: I didn't say so.

SPIJAK: You meant it.

ERIC: But you never heard me say it did you – ?

SPIJAK: Touch this for toughness, Eric. This'll last him a hundred years. Some yankee – big fancy hotel – stays in London – and gets copped for a hundred knicker for this, so it ought to last a hundred years.

ERIC: That's right you ruin the whole trade. You make up the suits like that and there'll be no clients left. Ain't you heard of built in obsolescence?

ERIC reaches for his jacket and waistcoat. He puts them on. He pulls on his overcoat and places his hat on his head.

SPIJAK: Where you going?

ERIC: You see – I don't need to work until midnight –

SPIJAK: Don't go like that –

ERIC: And for why – ?

SPIJAK: It's a bad image for the boy.

ERIC: I'm going home – play a nice classical record – and do meself a salmon salad with black olives –

SPIJAK is oddly nervous at ERIC leaving.

SPIJAK: Don't go – stay a bit Eric

He shows the brown jacket to ERIC.

SPIJAK: I just want to try it out. Just for me. Give it a go.

ERIC: What sort of a go?

SPIJAK: I'll doublepress it later – you can give it the works.

ERIC: I can?

SPIJAK: Go on.

ERIC takes the brown jacket and holds it up.

SPIJAK: Don't be afraid of it.

ERIC drops his hat. Suddenly, he screws the jacket up and starts beating it against the bench.

Harder than that.

ERIC takes the bottom of the jacket in his hand and flails it all over the benches – slap slap – with it.

Hundred years it will – Eric!

ERIC with a certain amount of glee takes the jacket and whacks it and whacks it all over the place.

Scrunch it up! Pull it about! Give it the works! Hundred years Eric!

ERIC: Not if I can help it!

ERIC is pummelling and bouncing the jacket for all he's got. He takes hand block and belts hell out of it.

SPIJAK: Stamp on it! Go on!

ERIC puts it on the ground and starts leaping and stamping on it.

Not like that! Pulverise it!

SPIJAK joins ERIC and they leap up and down together stamping and grinding the jacket into the ground. MAURICE bleakly watchers their antics.

Like this!... More! More!

They are stamping and kicking and lunging at the jacket. Until they are both exhausted by it. ERIC, with a degree of boyish pleasure, kicks the jacket up into SPIJAK's arms. SPIJAK holds up the jacket and stares at it. ERIC is breathing heavily.

SPIJAK: Look at that! ... One hundred years! ... When did you see such a jacket!...

Both men stand there panting. They are staring at each other and at the jacket.

Not a stitch out of true! Such a jacket...

ERIC: *(Nodding.)* Such a jacket…

> *He reaches for his hat and walks to the door. He turns –*

> … Night, lads.

SPIJAK: Don't go Eric…stay and work.

> *ERIC shakes his head. He opens the door. He leaves.*

> *SPIJAK and MAURICE get back to their work. SPIJAK dusts the brown coat down.*

> *The lights lower. An hour has passed. As the lights lift – MAURICE is hard at work sewing. SPIJAK snips and snaps with his shears.*

MAURICE: … How much more – ?

SPIJAK: Till I say, boy.

MAURICE: Excuse me – but I've made up until nine o'clock each night this work – it's –

SPIJAK: Work makes you forget…

MAURICE: But Spijak –

SPIJAK: Sir – lad.

MAURICE: *(With resolution.)* Spijak.

SPIJAK: Don't give me that. It's sir –

MAURICE: Not any more – it's Spijak.

SPIJAK: And what gives you that right? You're still speaking to me, boy!

> *MAURICE gets off the bench. He picks up the waistcoat he has been making from under the other jacket.*

MAURICE: … Some rights I have…somehow

> *He puts on the waistcoat and stands up in it.*

> That's my right. It's mine.

SPIJAK: Who gave you the cloth – ?

MAURICE: Sydie and Iris. Three and a half yards of it – and that's my right.

SPIJAK looking more closely at the waistcoat.

SPIJAK: Turn around…

MAURICE does.

What is it meant to be?

MAURICE: You can see.

SPIJAK: Well it approximately resembles a waistcoat.

MAURICE: That's what's my right.

SPIJAK sniffs loudly. He wipes his nose with his shirt sleeve.

SPIJAK: Not one machine stitch – ?

MAURICE: Not one.

SPIJAK shrugs and returns to his bench. He places a damp cloth on a panel on the press board. He lifts the iron and steam rises immediately the iron touches down.

SPIJAK: Bloody hell… Maurice.

MAURICE stands there in his waistcoat.

MAURICE: *(With a grin.)* Bloody hell… Spijak!

SPIJAK looks up. This time he says nothing. The steam rises beside him from the damp cloth. MAURICE stands before the tall mirror. He fingers the waistcoat.

The lights lower.

ACT TWO

It is a morning in June 1954. IRIS works at her boss's bench. SPIJAK stands at his bench. MAURICE sits at his.

MAURICE: … Sydie's late …

IRIS: She's got the morning off…

MAURICE: Well, where's she gone – ?

SPIJAK: Here Maurice…you can make turn back cuffs. But shrink the under-lay.

MAURICE: Spijak –

SPIJAK: Like Iris says – that's all.

MAURICE: Cuffs is for a kipper.

SPIJAK: Are you arguing – ?

MAURICE: I'm not arguing.

SPIJAK: Fine then.

MAURICE: I'd just like to be told why nobody will tell me why no one ain't here.

IRIS: Do you know – I've got pigeons in my backyard now… they're sitting on the loo seat in the outshot.

SPIJAK is a different man. He has an enforced gaiety about him. A nervousness underlies it all.

MAURICE: These cuffs…cuffs are still for a kipper, Spijak.

SPIJAK: I'll tell you what I'll do – leave them alone I'll do them – you can baste these forearms in – and if they hang right – you can sew them yourself. And you can finish make them.

SPIJAK hands the sleeves and the finished jacket over to the boy. SPIJAK goes to the rolley and takes down another jacket which is hanging close to ERIC's bench.

IRIS: … Blimey…

SPIJAK: What's that for Iris – ?

IRIS: You must be feeling ill –

SPIJAK: Maurice is no cack-handed boy no more – he can make up semi-finish.

IRIS: Long as I've lived I've never seen you hand out sleeve heads to finish to a boy –

SPIJAK: You can do it, can't you boy –

MAURICE: Maurice –

SPIJAK: That's right – I'm sorry – Maurice. Well can you or can't you – ?

MAURICE: I know how to, but –

IRIS: He's never done it before –

MAURICE: Do me a favour Iris – I'm telling him I can do it.

SPIJAK takes the coat from the rolley back to his bench.

SPIJAK: Course you can. Nine months with me and you're almost an artist. I'd trust you with anything bar nothing. I might not trust you with a roll collar but how often do we see that? And Eric and Iris ain't seen a roll collar dinner jacket since the beginning of time. Why's that? Because the guv' nor upstairs know you can't shove that work under a machine. That sort of work is damp-pressed and finger-rolled until it's a work of art.

IRIS: Shame…

SPIJAK: It's true. You and Eric ought to admit that.

IRIS: If you're going to run down Eric in absence, I'm going to talk about my pigeons.

SPIJAK: Please…be merciful.

The internal phone rings. MAURICE looks up towards SPIJAK but SPIJAK looks down. IRIS lays her work on the bench and crosses to the phone.

IRIS: … Iris… Eric's Iris… Oh no sir, yes sir no sir – well he won't be back before – He'll have to rush it…how? I'll run it over meself won't I? …

She puts the phone back. She returns to her side of ERIC's bench.

SPIJAK: What you got there Iris?

IRIS: It's a skiffle.

SPIJAK: Bad is it – ?

IRIS: Make up and second fit by lunch time – and the facings aren't down yet. Even Eric can't do that.

MAURICE: Shame…

The door is kicked open suddenly and the RUNNER throws the bundles into the room. Three are for ERIC.

RUNNER: … Eric!

First bundle wings its way on to ERIC's bench. IRIS tries to catch it.

RUNNER: … Eric!

The second.

RUNNER: … Eric!

SPIJAK: What about Spijak?

RUNNER: *(A beat then.)* … Maurice!

The bundle flies towards MAURICE's head. He, with some surprise, catches it. The door slams shut. The foot-steps retreat. MAURICE stares at the bundle.

MAURICE: They got the wrong Maurice.

SPIJAK: Open it.

MAURICE rips the brown paper. He pulls out a pair of finished trousers the colour of the waistcoat he made for himself.

MAURICE: When did I make these – ?

SPIJAK: Course you never made them – they're your'n. Put them on. You making that suit for yourself, aren't you? I took the material – cut it myself – and sent it down East for you. No self-respecting tailor makes trousers up does he? It's all kipper work.

MAURICE stands up and keeps to the far side of the bench away from both SPIJAK and IRIS and puts the trousers on. He comes up front. They are a good fit.

SPIJAK: Do they fit or don't they – ?

MAURICE: They fit.

SPIJACK: Course they fit. I borrowed an old pattern. Did the rest from eye. What a fit they are.

MAURICE: I don't understand you. What's the matter with you today – ?

SPIJAK: Nothing is –

MAURICE: You can't keep this up all day – being so pleasant I mean. It's twelve o'clock in the morning and you haven't once yet lost your conkers. Do you need a doctor – ?

SPIJAK: Don't lip me like that I was –

MAURICE: The telephone rings it's not for you –

SPIJAK: It never is, don't you know that –

MAURICE: The runner dollops down three make-ups for Eric and nothing for us – and you're still smiling.

MAURICE goes back behind the bench and takes off the trousers.

SPIJAK: Well go on – thank me.

MAURICE: Thank you.

SPIJAK: There you are then – it's for free.

MAURICE: You're not going to give me the sack are you?

SPIJAK: Nobody's a bleeding tyrant every waking moment –

MAURICE: Sometimes you give a pretty good impression of it –

SPIJAK: I want to see you finish that suit. I'll give you free time in the evenings – you finish it down to the last and I'll get Sydie to button-hole it –

MAURICE: She's already said –

SPIJAK: And I'll give it a special press up and damp out. When a boy's made his first suit for his-self he's done his learning. What's the perks Iris for a boy when he makes up all his own – ?

IRIS: Boy don't do any more running up front shop with jobs –

SPIJAK: That's right.

IRIS: And the boy don't make no tea anymore –

SPIJAK: And all kipper work goes back to the kipper. Right – ?

IRIS nods. MAURICE climbs back on to his bench.

MAURICE: I thought you hated my guts.

SPIJAK: Because I wanted you to be a craftsman – ? I love you, boy. I want you to make up better than me – and I want you to make up better than the other two hundred makers in this lousy profession. And I don't care how long it takes you to make – you'll learn to be that good, you can hold a finished jacket in your hands, and you could be blindfolded, you'd still feel it was perfect make. It's in your fingers then – its balance and its finish and its rightness: – there are some finishes you just need to touch to know it's best making. Only you need to know that. Nobody else will. You'll make best, Maurice. I'll see…

At the sound of the steps down the outside stairs, SPIJAK becomes silent. IRIS looks up. She follows SPIJAK's gaze. The door opens and ERIC, dressed in a dark suit and a black hat walks into the room.

SPIJAK: … Afternoon, Eric.

ERIC: Morning…

SPIJAK: It's going to be what you call a long day isn't it – ?

ERIC: Imagine so…

ERIC slowly takes off his hat and coat. He rolls up his sleeves with a meticulous style.

IRIS: Mr. Stanbury was on the phone. I spoke to him.

SPIJAK: Yes, the phone rang Eric.

ERIC: Thanks.

SPIJAK: Yes, the phone rang. Course I didn't answer it. Weren't much use in me answering it. He don't want to talk to me now…does he – ?

ERIC: Perhaps he does perhaps he doesn't.

SPIJAK: *(But with as much charm as he can muster.)* So it doesn't ring… Boss knows the quickest maker in this side of Dover Street and –

ERIC: Spijak!

SPIJAK: Straight out I mean. In all honesty I mean – and I'm not pulling the wool – you're it Eric. I mean I know I bullshit about you and the machine – but you know it's not for real – I appreciate the way you work. I'm not knocking. You're an artist – you may be a fast artist – but you're an artist.

ERIC: Iris – what did Mr. Louis want – ?

SPIJAK: Fact is – all along – I'm prepared to admit, it's no use making up my way. It's too slow. Look at my wage packet – why is it always half of your'n – not because I'm more worse maker than you – but because I don't see reason. It's your built-in obsolescence don't you call it?

IRIS: There's a make-up and second fit by lunch time – and we ain't got the facings down on it yet.

ERIC: Strike me…

IRIS: So I said I don't know – I said we'd have to run it over ourselves – but I said I wasn't to know what time you'd be back.

ERIC: *(Looking around.)* Where is the jacket then – ?

IRIS and ERIC sift through all the bundles on the bench. It is not there. ERIC skims through the jackets hanging on the rolley. He cannot find it.

ERIC: That's impossible…

IRIS: I saw it last night…

SPIJAK makes a loud humming noise and snaps cotton through his teeth after a final stitch. ERIC glances across at the jacket SPIJAK is working on, it is ERIC's rush job jacket. SPIJAK knows he has seen it. He hums away in a kind of self-deprecating manner, ERIC goes across the room to him –

ERIC: Spijak – ?

SPIJAK: Yes – ?

ERIC: What's this – ?

ERIC lifts up the near finished jacket and holds it up to the light.

ERIC: That's my making –

SPIJAK: Is it – ?

ERIC: That's my jacket you're touching.

SPIJAK: Stitch me – is it?

SPIJAK looks mock wide-eyed as ERIC pulls the jacket away.

ERIC: What are you doing finishing off my work?

SPIJAK: Well, to be honest –

ERIC: I don't want you to be honest. I'd rather you was your normal unpleasant self.

SPIJAK: I heard Iris on the phone – and knowing not knowing the time you'd be back like she said – and thinking you had this great skiffle on –

ERIC: How dare you make up on mine!

SPIJAK: I'm doing you a favour. There you are – not there at all – and you got a rush job on.

ERIC: Nobody makes up for anybody else in this trade –

SPIJAK: But seeing –

ERIC: You ain't got the right to touch this. This is mine. I don't want all your finger marks down my gussets.

SPIJAK: I thought you'd thank me –

ERIC: When have you ever done me a favour before? It's not that I'm talking about. What I'm saying is – I never gave you the permission. Look what he's done, Iris – he's –

IRIS: Shame…

ERIC: He's done his handstitching down my facings –

IRIS: Blinking liberty –

ERIC: I don't want to take no handstitching down the facings into the front shop – they'll say hallo, Eric's gone mad.

MAURICE: Course they might just reckon your machine broke down.

ERIC: Point is – it's poaching.

SPIJAK: I thought you'd thank me –

ERIC: Ain't you got work enough?

SPIJAK: Don't be like that – I'm your friend aren't I?
I'm helping you out.

IRIS: Eric and me don't need it.

SPIJAK: Everybody does – needs help.

ERIC takes the jacket and reluctantly inspects it. It has indeed been finished off rather well by SPIJAK for a second fit with sewn facings.

SPIJAK: *(Softly.)* … Even I need a bit of help sometimes.

ERIC looks up slowly. There is a dawning in his mind.

ERIC: Funny you never asked me where I went this morning – ?

SPIJAK: Well, go on – aren't you going to press that jacket off then?

ERIC: Funny you never mentioned what day it was today – ?

SPIJAK: Run it up will you – and I'll send Maurice over to the shop with it – special favour.

ERIC: Never asked you did he Iris – ?

IRIS: Don't bring me into it.

SPIJAK: *(Helplessly.)* You could be nice to me Eric – you could thank me for that finish on the facings

ERIC: Where was I then – ?

SPIJAK: I don't know, I –

ERIC: You know –

SPIJAK: Please –

ERIC: You know!

SPIJAK: All right …!

ERIC: … I wanted to hear you say that.

Both men attack their individual work with sudden energy, ERIC wets his damp-cloth and squeezes it, and flaps the loose water over the floor.

ERIC: … Wasn't I in Kensal Rise, Spijak?

SPIJAK won't answer.

ERIC: Wasn't I dressed in me black and in me dark hat wasn't I?

SPIJAK: *(Ignoring. To MAURICE.)* Dampcloth all of that back seam and press it out. As much water as you can –

ERIC: You remember Kensal Rise Cemetery…remember all of six years ago?

SPIJAK: I'm not listening –

ERIC: But I'm speaking. Wasn't that the day you shouted all through the service. Shouted before you stepped inside and you never stopped until the little curtain slipped aside and that box slid away.

IRIS: Leave him…!

ERIC: Mary was half as much your wife as she was my sister, she was.

ERIC sneezes quickly. He pulls out a handkerchief and blows his nose.

SPIJAK: *(Sleep-walking, really.)* And you don't do that anymore you don't. That famous sneeze of your'n. Remember that sneeze you could do – tell Maurice Iris – Eric could sneeze so loud we used to think he was going to do his chest no end of damage. Until we discovered it wasn't just a sneeze – Eric could sneeze and fart at the same time – isn't that true? What a noise! Cross between a thunderclap and a Japanese firecracker!

ERIC: You don't want to remember what day it is today. If you can call a death an anniversary –

SPIJAK: And Iris would say – that was in the days when she was new on the bench and a bit on the feared side of Eric – she'd say strewth and houses Mr. Eric light a match someone there's a terrible smell in here!

ERIC: And you don't want to ask me – did I see Sydie there? Did she and I put flowers on the little marble box set in the wall? Did we sit down and have a talk about the old days? Did we talk about you? Say how she might have lived if –

IRIS: Eric stop it!

SPIJAK: You used to fart and sneeze once you did –

ERIC: I'll tell you – we never sat down and asked each other why wasn't there? Why you never have been back?

SPIJAK pulls himself up on his bench to work cross-legged. MAURICE lays out the spread back seam for a very heavy damping with the large iron.

SPIJAK: Just put the weight of the iron dead centre – lean on it –

MAURICE lifts the iron and slams it down heavily. The steam rises up with a sharp hiss.

ERIC: I loved her, and if I'd had the sense to love her proper like a brother should I'd never have allowed her in this trade. She met you and she believed all that rubbish about good making – and it was fourteen hours a day – six days a week – and she never gave up because she believed that was real making. That was craft, she believed. And it bloody killed her. I take that back. It wasn't craft what killed her. What did it was how you never understood. She was a weak little tiny bird in your hand and she thought she'd found a hero. It was Spijak who thought he was the greatest maker on God's earth.

Unwatched by either SPIJAK or ERIC, MAURICE stands with his hands glued to the heavy iron over the seams. Less steam rises now.

SPIJAK: I never thought you'd have that much lack of decency to bring up all – that you'd do this in front of others – I get an apprentice I'm training – my Father's Father died on a bench in Warsaw dropped and died and died happy doing what he could do best – say to me you loved her – not saying to me at all you are – you mean I never gave

Mary a proper home – that it was one lousy set of rooms to another – saying to me you are I had no right to tell her I wanted to make well and make better than it's ever thought possible to – well she was born to it.

ERIC: My father made me swear she'd never wind up on a kipper's bench with fingers like bloody raisins –

SPIJAK: I was trying to be nice – Maurice here give him a cut of his trousers for his suit – tacked up facings like you'd never hope to see such facings account of you're ashamed of good work – had me a boss what made me breathe in fear of the living day – to be a playboy Spijak you have to learn to do one thing well just one and better than the best anybody else can – and in those days you believed him. I come in in the morning – baste bundle down on the bench – open it with crying terror – sew it and make it that fine – out of crying fear out of anger because it hurts – that it be right. Say to me it's easy – the machine – nothing lives but out of fear – cannot feel a piece of cloth until it aches to touch it – cannot live without it hurting – if my soul bleeds like fingers cut and bleed I know I am yet alive!

ERIC: That's right – get it off your chest – go on man –

SPIJAK: Don't tell me I'm guilty about Mary – or tell it in front of Iris – I'm told in myself I am – and I'm praying dear God am I – I'm sitting up and begging on the Torah and in holy fear of my being and seeing the Dybbuk in my hands when I work wrong – and God help me if I'm not reading from memory of my father's and hearing the first six books of the Old Testament –

MAURICE: There are five books in the Pentateuch –

SPIJAK: So one book more don't make no harm – do it! There's a Tailor Eric – and you may have trouble to find him – there's the Greatest Tailor of them all in this *schmut in mitske derinnen* – one who's got His eye dead centre in the needle – believe me Heaven come up – you stand there – I'm machine mad Eric from Kilgours – and He looks at your suit – don't expect Him to let you in on a second, third or fourth fitting Eric – God's Heavenly Great Wonders is no baste job runner's sprint up Sackville Street!

ERIC is banging away with his handblock. Swinging his arm.

It is noticeable that MAURICE's iron no longer sends up smoke from his damp cloth.

SPIJAK: Don't say guilty to me – I know it I got it – as clear as you can tell the difference between horsehair and a lump of velvet –

ERIC: That's more like the old Spijak? Ain't that true Iris?

SPIJAK: *(Sniffing.)* What's that – ?

MAURICE: What's what – ?

SPIJAK: *(Lifting his nose.)* What's in my nose.

MAURICE: What is in your nose then – ?

SPIJAK stares at the iron MAURICE has not moved from the seam.

SPIJAK: I don't see no smoke rising from your damp cloth

MAURICE lifts the iron away. An acrid black smoke rises from the cloth.

MAURICE: Oh Gawd…!

MAURICE lifts the twin back panels up – there is one clear cut out shape of a burnt iron-sized hole in the centre of the back.

SPIJAK: Well I'm telling you – it'll take a year yet or more to turn you into a playboy!

MAURICE: I'm sorry I –

SPIJAK: And it'll take me a month or more before I call you anything but boy, too! You're going straight back into the realm of fear, boy!

SPIJAK reaches for his coat. He stands by the door.

MAURICE: Spijak – I'm sorry –

SPIJAK: You got fear and trembling boy – just like when you
began – until I forget!

MAURICE: Spijak!

*SPIJAK is out of the door. The door slams behind him. His footsteps
retreat up to the street.*

*MAURICE angrily throws the ruined panels on to the bench. He leans
his head on the bench and draws in deep breaths.*

IRIS: … It was you – Eric …

ERIC: Is it him alone what's only supposed to have feelings – ?

IRIS: … Summer holidays is coming up soon …

ERIC: True enough.

IRIS: Got me eye on a little wooden bungalow at Herne Bay
– right on the sand it is…and at night when the sea sends
up them breezes – you only have to leave the screen porch
door loose and it'll bang away all night. But in the morning
there are sea-gulls and I lay out my bread on a sheet of
brown paper. Their beaks go snap snap snap – and when
it rains, I put on a thick woolly and take my sandals off by
the shallow. Water's always warmer after it has rained.

*MAURICE is still. He keeps his position. ERIC takes down another
job from the rolley. He holds on to his nose for a moment. But he
can't stop the sneeze. He gasps, and then at one – farts and sneezes
at the same time. Thunder-clap. IRIS reaches inside her handbag she
pulls out a box of matches.*

IRIS: There's a terrific smell in here…

ERIC: I wasn't going to let Spijak have the benefit of that one.

IRIS strikes a match, holds her nose, and wafts the match in the air.

IRIS: Strike a light …shame …

The lights lower. The room is dark in the tiled passage to the lavatory cubicle the lights lift. MAURICE is sitting on the seat, on his knees is a writing pad. The door is shut and locked. SYDIE, in a coat and hat, enters. She tries the door. It won't open. She has a large handbag on her arm.

SYDIE: … Hurry up, Iris – !

MAURICE: It ain't Iris.

SYDIE: I'm in a hurry.

MAURICE: Cross your legs.

She takes out a packet of sandwiches and places them beside the door on the floor.

SYDIE: They're banana…

MAURICE: Fine.

SYDIE: …and cheese and pickle.

MAURICE: Thanks.

SYDIE: I don't know what you do in there – every day every lunch time –

MAURICE: It's quiet in here.

SYDIE: Never occurs to you I suppose somebody else might want to use the –

MAURICE: It's quiet – and it's cool in here – and nobody is shouting.

SYDIE: If it's not a rude question – just what do you find to do – ?

MAURICE: Nothing –

SYDIE: You can't do –

MAURICE: I write…a little.

SYDIE: Sit in the bog every lunch and write words what for do you want to do that?

MAURICE: Would you understand if I say I can tell myself
what I'm thinking – ?

SYDIE: By writing!

MAURICE: By writing for Christ's sake!

*MAURICE opens the door. Pushes it that much forward, and watches
her.*

SYDIE: … You don't belong in this trade.

MAURICE: My Father cut – his Father made up somewhere
on the south coast – I have a great-aunt who showed me
a picture of her Father's brother – he was employed as
a kind of living Tailor's dummy, in Leeds. Wore the best
suits, the firm made him a club member, and he went
racing with the bespoke crowd. That was his job.

SYDIE: But it's dying. Nobody really wants craft. The rich want
craft. Nobody else. The guv'nor don't want my Father
working that bench. He's too slow. They want a maker
who can knock up four second fittings in a week. You can't
become a Spijak when your learning's up.

MAURICE: Did you see Eric in Kensal Rise?

SYDIE: We laid the flowers together.

MAURICE: You loved her, didn't you – ?

SYDIE: No concern of –

MAURICE: You won't even tell him you've got a fellow –
he's in some kind of mass produced rubbish in fifty shilling
Tailors – and I know you won't. You're so afraid
of him you'd let him walk over you.

SYDIE: That's the way I prefer it.

MAURICE: Your Father collects that pathetic pay packet
every week – he's never home with you before two in
the morning – every morning – cut out of his skull with
boozing and you won't stand up to it. No use saying to me

I'll never make a maker – you'll never speak the truth to
him.

SYDIE: You keep to your little Mother in her council flat
– and I'll keep to my tyrant in there.

MAURICE: I'll stay.

SYDIE: You won't. Come a morning – wake up – say to
yourself what am I doing stitching my fingers off their
joints – there's an easier life than –

MAURICE: Maybe I like the way he says it's got to hurt.

SYDIE: Most boys take their National Service like lemmings
– when they come out – like Mickey did – they're not
looking for a bench and a kipper and a pair of goose irons
they're looking for twenty pound a week and a pension.
Don't kid yourself there's a pension up there waiting for
my Father or Eric –

*MAURICE stands up. He laconically pulls the lavatory chain.
It flushes.*

MAURICE: It's free now.

SYDIE: You're just like Mickey – you'll go. You won't come
back.

*He walks out. She enters the cubicle and shuts the door. The lights
lower immediately.*

*It is the afternoon of a day, late in December, 1954, IRIS is out of the
room. SPIJAK is under his bench. Occasionally he snores. MAURICE
and SYDIE are standing inside a huge double-breasted jacket which
ERIC lifts and pushes at the shoulders to get a balance to hang. They
face the mirror. Each has an arm down a sleeve.*

MAURICE: … This geezer's trousers must look like a sleeping
bag for two.

ERIC: Hold still –

SYDIE: Wonder the bobbin didn't fall off your machine Eric.

ERIC: Big man this –

MAURICE: Hardly likely to be Gordon Richards' grand-stand bib and tucker is it?

ERIC: *(Fussing.)* Big man in the theatre he is –

SYDIE: If I was him I'd be in the circus.

ERIC: Henry Sherek this is. Mr. Sherek the impresario this is. First nights in Piccadilly with the stars.

SYDIE: Well where we going then – ?

ERIC: Going to Oddenino's. Or the Mirabelle after the applause has died down. Good evening Mr. Sherek was the house full?

MAURICE: I'd say it was – he had a whole row of seats to himself.

MAURICE and SYDIE reach for a stool, they put themselves down on it.

SYDIE: Well what'll it be – ?

MAURICE: It'll be four chump chops and a double plate meat tartar – rare!

ERIC: Careful!

There is a terrible rending sound at the back. SYDIE and MAURICE look over their shoulders.

ERIC: Watch it!

MAURICE: There's a terrible rending sound at the back, Eric!

SYDIE: Blimey, Eric!

They pull away from each other, the whole back seam and its lining has slit adrift.

ERIC: Go easy!

MAURICE: You been putting cotton wool on the machine again Eric!

ERIC pulls them out of the jacket. He undoes the buttons. And holds up the tattered jacket. MAURICE and SYDIE crease themselves.

SYDIE: You can't have em' walking out of Oddenino's like that!

MAURICE and SYDIE return to their benches. ERIC twists the jacket inside out and glumly carries it back.

ERIC: … Something wrong with that needle in that machine commence work.

MAURICE and SYDIE choke their laughter as they commence work.

The light lifts on the lavatory downstairs. IRIS opens the cubicle door and pulls the chain. She walks up to the room. The lights lower on the tiled corner. IRIS opens the side door and walks to her place at the side of ERIC's bench.

ERIC: *(To IRIS.)* What you been doing down there – taking your summer holidays!

SYDIE: Shame…

IRIS: Blinking nerve…

ERIC: What with you and Maurice – why don't you both move in down there – take a hot water bottle – if I was the guv'nor I'd put a cabbie's clock down there.

IRIS: Is that your pile of papers you keep down behind the lav Maurice?

MAURICE: It might be.

IRIS: Well, in any case there's a chronic shortage of loo paper down there –

MAURICE: Iris you haven't been tearing up my writings and using it for your bum?

IRIS: How dare you!

MAURICE: Well that's my play that is –

IRIS: I got better things to do than wipe my arse with your play I have.

ERIC: Shut up Iris – and get on.

They all put their heads down and work. After a pause, MAURICE looks up.

MAURICE: *(To SYDIE.)* First year I came here – had a half pint in the French Pub on Dean Street – and there's this famous poet I was standing next to –

SYDIE: Never heard of him –

MAURICE: I ain't told you his name yet have I?

SYDIE: Don't know what you'll catch standing beside poets in the French Pub.

MAURICE: Dylan Thomas he was. Fat and plastered he was and reciting out loud.

SYDIE: What did you do – offer him a cheap baste job?

MAURICE: Stood up next to him and spoke to him.

SYDIE: How do you do, I'm Maurice the tailor – I got a play downstairs in the workroom bog what I'm trying to keep the kippers from wiping their bums on!

MAURICE: He never actually replied to me. Surrounded by artists though. Painters and boozers and writers. They didn't speak to me either. Can't just really walk up to them like that.

SYDIE: But Maurice – just what do you think you are going to do with a play what you keep in the bog over there behind the lav – ?

MAURICE: Course if I had Eric's contacts with the theatrical stage and screen – I could show it to Mr Sherek.

IRIS: Eric's awfully fond of cultural things.

ERIC: I got the last ticket for the Opera Christmas Eve.

IRIS: Eric likes good music.

ERIC: I like a nice hot bath with a bit of the old Puccini
knocking the lid off my gramophone

IRIS: Eric's got a very good gramophone.

ERIC: Decca it is – genuine mahogany box.

IRIS: Always polishing it aren't you?

ERIC: La Traviata – that's what gets me. Clean pyjamas – hot
cup of cocoa – La Traviata and the Racing Gazette, and
I'm sleeping like an empty bobbin.

*The phone by the wall starts to ring. SPIJAK wakes suddenly. He bangs
his head against the underside of the bench. He lies back with a groan.*

ERIC: *(To SPIJAK.)* Don't you worry yourself none – it ain't for
you.

As he makes for the phone. SPIJAK slowly climbs to his feet.

ERIC: *(At the mouthpiece.)* Yes sir – Eric sir – how many! By
New Year! All of them! Yes sir, you can rely on me can't
you sir. I see…well you can only try… Christmas holidays
start tomorrow…don't you fret sir. *(He puts the phone down.)*
… Stitch me.

SPIJAK: Who's in the shop Eric – the Three Wise Men – ?

ERIC: Robert Taylor no less.

SPIJAK: Who?

ERIC: Robert Taylor walks in the shop with two executives
from MGM and orders fifty suits! Fifty!

SPIJAK: Never heard of him.

ERIC: Robert Taylor – did you never see *Gone With The Wind?*
Fifty make ups and I've got ten of them. Including a roll

collar dj. Who was it who said the front shop'd never give me a roll collar – Robert Taylor, mate, that's who!

SPIJAK throws pieces around his board. There is little on the board.

SPIJAK: … What we got, Maurice – ?

MAURICE: Nothing …

SPIJAK: Sydie – ?

SYDIE: These are last pockets.

SPIJAK sweeps a pile of clutter off the bench all across the floor.

ERIC: All skiffles – finish by January 6th.

IRIS: Have to pull out fingers out won't we? After the holidays.

ERIC: You taking some home with you I'm telling.

IRIS: Ooh…

SPIJAK: Just itching ain't you Eric – get down on the machine just itching to.

ERIC: *(Softly.)* I'm sorry mate…but that's how it goes don't it …

The front door is kicked open, the RUNNER throws the small brown wage packets across the room. They roughly go in the right direction. All the kippers and tailors have to move to catch them.

RUNNER: Pay day! … Catch it! … Happy Christmas!

As he shuts the door quickly, SPIJAK hurls a whole handblock after him at the door.

SPIJAK: Get off!

The RUNNER's quick steps up to the road outside.

They all open their packets.

SYDIE: … What you got Iris – ?

IRIS: Nine pound fourteen shilling and nine pence.

SYDIE: Three bob more'n me.

ERIC: *(Opening his.)* That's the first time this whole I been over twenty. Look at that – Iris – twenty-one pound six and eightpence halfpenny.

SPIJAK opens his.

SPIJAK: Fourteen exactly.

SPIJAK throws the packet on the bench ERIC is silent for a while.

ERIC: *(A beat; then softly.)* … Spijak – ?

SPIJAK: *(Barely audible.)* Happy Christmas, Eric.

ERIC: *(Banging his block.)* Yearh…happy Christmas

SPIJAK looks all around him. At SYDIE and MAURICE. IRIS purposefully looks away and down at her work. SPIJAK goes across to the phone. He hesitates. The others turn to watch him. SPIJAK whirls the handle on the side of the phone and lifts the speaker –

SPIJAK: … This is Spijak … No! Spijak in the Dover Street room. Remember? … Those eh – film star jobs – them skiffles – I know I know, don't tell me you never give me skiffles. Have you placed them all? … I'm saying I will aren't I? I'm saying I can. Yes – please – that's right. No hand finish. All machine. There won't be a handstitch on the fucking lot! My name's Spijak – I'll spell it. S–P–I–J …

He puts the phone on its hook. Slowly he walks to the bench.

ERIC: *(A beat; then.)* … Spijak.

SPIJAK: Yes, Eric – ?

ERIC: Happy Christmas, lad.

IRIS: *(To SYDIE.)* Funny to be working so hard over holidays init – ?

SYDIE: Funny, Iris?

She stands up and slams her materials down on the bench. Her eyes rim with tears. She walks out to the downstairs washroom.

… For Christ's sake it ain't funny is it!

She bangs the side door behind her.

MAURICE is looking up at SPIJAK.

MAURICE: … You never had to do that.

SPIJAK: Shall I show you my wage packet again?

MAURICE: What have you been saying all these months to me?

SPIJAK: What I think is right is all I've been saying.

MAURICE: You're impressed aren't you? Eric's finally got through. He had a Ford Anglia last Christmas now he's got a Vauxhall Victor. What have you got – you got three rooms over a hair-dressing saloon in Billericay and –

SPIJAK: You just stick to what you think I've taught you –

MAURICE: Eric's house is his – he bought it didn't he?

SPIJAK: I don't stand for no mortgage –

MAURICE: Course you don't, it's usury ain't it? It's your hocking yourself and your selling yourself and your robbing yourself –

SPIJAK: That's right.

MAURICE: But I could do six months on assembly work at Montague Burton to polish off a dozen film star's skiffles, couldn't I?

SPIJAK: Are you asking?

MAURICE: I'm stating.

SPIJAK: I can't hear you!

MAURICE: Well that's it. That's the end of another year.

MAURICE throws all the work down and gets off the bench. He rolls down his sleeves and reaches for his jacket.

SPIJAK: Where are you going?

MAURICE: Home, sir –

SPIJAK: Don't call me sir –

MAURICE: Yes sir – home sir – I'll see you after Christmas sir –

SPIJAK: What about this film star work – ?

MAURICE: Work, sir? That ain't work –

SPIJAK: Maurice I need you –

MAURICE: Call that work? That's not work – that's Austin Reed con shop bullshit that's Jacksons of Savile Row that's your Simpsons drip dry don't count the stitches feel the price!

SPIJAK: I can't make up without you –

MAURICE: And you can't put the fright of God up me without me.

SPIJAK: Five days – that's all –

MAURICE: No sir. You won't kill me off on a machine. My life on it!

MAURICE takes his macintosh from the wall and walks out the door.

MAURICE: Iris and Eric – happy Christmas!

The door shuts behind him. His footsteps fade away.

IRIS: *(A beat. Then.)* … Happy Christmas.

SPIJAK puts his hand down and sews away. IRIS and ERIC work closely together on one piece of cloth. Seconds pass by.

ERIC: *(To IRIS.)* … Nice bit of turkey and raspberry jam – me foot up on the – Decca Black Box – and Vivaldi on the long play – that's what I look forward to.

IRIS: I could bring you round a piece of me own Christmas pudding. Cream sauce with brandy.

ERIC: Oh no – always make me own. I do a soft milk trifle with sherry top it with cherries. Just right with the –

SPIJAK: You're a poof you are.

ERIC: I didn't hear that.

SPIJAK: Screaming pansified pince poncing give us a wink raving poof.

ERIC: How dare you – ?

SPIJAK: Why didn't you never marry – ?

ERIC: More sense I have –

SPIJAK: You're a right wincing poof Eric!

IRIS: Shame …

SPIJAK: A poof a do it yourself on the machine play a piece of raving nancy classical music poof you are!

ERIC: Want me to take my scissors to you – ?

ERIC waves his shears at SPIJAK.

SPIJAK: A Decca Black Box thirty-three and a third long playing poof!

IRIS: My Eric's not a poof!

SPIJAK: Course he is!

ERIC: I'll cut your gonads off!

SPIJAK: So long as I've known you –

As ERIC approaches SPIJAK snip-snapping his shears at him, SPIJAK reaches for his shears – and they square up at each other waving their shears –

SPIJAK: Baste poof and second finish machine collar poof!

ERIC: But I never killed no one!

SPIJAK: Just a nancy's nark!

ERIC: I ain't never killed off the thing I most loved!

SPIJAK, his shears aimed at ERIC's parts, pauses, he stands back and stares at ERIC. ERIC holds his shears at the ready.

As they stand there – poised –

The door to the front steps is kicked open.

RUNNER: Eric! … Eric? …

As the bundles start flying in through the air.

RUNNER: Spijak! … Spijak!

Twenty bundles start flying through the air at great speed.

RUNNER: Eric! … Spijak! … Eric! … Spijak!

SPIJAK and ERIC race up and down the room to catch them all, They collide. They turn around – to catch the bundles as they keep on coming through the door at them. The door slams again.

RUNNER'S VOICE: … Happy Christmas!

Both SPIJAK and ERIC have collected so many of the bundles in their arms, they reel back into one another and collapse in a heap in the centre of the room.

SPIJAK and ERIC are surrounded by the bundles. They each grasp as many as they can. They climb up off the floor holding on their own.

SPIJAK fumbles with his bundles. He picks one out –

SPIJAK: …who's got the roll collar job!

IRIS: Shame …

SPIJAK: *(With triumph.)* I got it! … I have!

ERIC throws a bundle at SPIJAK. SPIJAK throws one back at him. It becomes a pillow fight. They run up and down the room – ducking and diving – one bundle after the other flies through the air.

They will not stop. They throw and throw at each other. The bundles crash across the benches. IRIS ducks.

The lights lower.

It is later in the evening. As the lights lift, only the fluorescent tube above SPIJAK's bench is on. SYDIE sits apposite him. SPIJAK makes up.

SYDIE: … Why don't you use the machine then – ?

SPIJAK: Later.

SYDIE: I've got all these side seams ready, as well as the back seams.

SPIJAK: I'll do it.

SYDIE: You won't get this lot done in five days – you know it. Unless we use the machine –

SPIJAK: Just go home Sydie.

SYDIE: You come, too.

SPIJAK: You got that boy-friend, right – ? Well, ask him over. Give him supper, Christmas Eve.

SYDIE: That'll be the day.

SPIJAK: I'll stay here. I got plenty here for me.

SYDIE: All Christmas! When I've fetched all that shopping –

SPIJAK: Don't whitewash, girl. It'll be a better holiday without me. Ain't it true – ?

SYDIE: I might go to a dance with Charlie – He'll fetch me back – mince pies and a spot of that brandy.

SPIJAK: You do that.

SYDIE: I might marry him you know –

SPIJAK: So suddenly you're married.

SYDIE: Well?

SPIJAK: When I married your mother I had one baste waist-coat on the bench, and I shared a kipper with four other makers. She worked Mary did – she'd do more'n me and half again if she had the strength.

SYDIE: She didn't.

SPIJAK: What we wanted was one little shop. Before you were born. We'd make a suit every twelve days – each make up would be a Tailor & Cutter annual award – so good they'd last an hundred year. Course it never happened –

SYDIE: It's only a suit –

SPIJAK: That's what Eric says – and he's a butcher he's got the morals of a butcher.

SYDIE stands. She takes off her apron and reaches for her coat.

SPIJAK: And Sydie –

SYDIE: Yes.

SPIJAK: I ain't never killed no one.

SYDIE: You don't have to –

SPIJAK: Work don't kill.

SYDIE: All right.

SPIJAK: Love of craft don't – knowing you can do something better'n anybody else in all Dover Street don't – believing if it's got to be right it's got to be perfect don't –

She kisses him quickly on his face.

SYDIE: I'll see you when I see you –

SPIJAK: See – I got good straight hands I got eyes tell a true line better'n any machine – and your mother know that too – to honour the gifts the Great Tailor first gave –

SYDIE: Happy Christmas, mate.

SPIJAK: It ain't happiness you need …

SYDIE: Shall I expect you – ?

SPIJAK: Day you start looking for happiness day you start dying you do.

SYDIE: T'rra

She shuts the outside door behind her. Her steps fade away.

The lights change. It is much later. In early morning hours. SPIJAK is working. He is tired.

n.b – the underlined passages signify the present.

SPIJAK: … Go home too, Mary. You go on. I can finish. What for want – stay as late as this want – and you just back from our honeymoon. I ain't going to work you. Didn't I promise? That was a perfect honeymoon – and that's the truth of the word. Every minute of it was. Remember that Boys Brigade hut on the beach – back there of the sand dunes – and you were saying 'I can hear that door squeaking sure as sin someone might walk in and see us like this – oh God!' If anything was squeaking it was that rotten mattress girl. 'Spijak! You're so coarse'!' But you laughed… <u>Perhaps you didn't laugh, perhaps…</u>

He reaches for a crate of bottles beneath his bench.

… 'And you keep your oath now, that you'll never drink again, Spijak?'… That's right girl that's my word.

He lifts out a half finished bottle of vodka and takes a pull at it.

…and you won't be kippering none more than I can help. You'll see. Take a while. Small place. Shop with our own name. And we'll be sixty or seventy strolling – then there's this nine ounce double-breasted coming up Bond Street towards us, young as we made it the day it first felt shoulder blades<u>… I never told you about that honeymoon</u>… But if it takes me ten years to train a boy to make as well as us – you'll never work again, I swear… <u>And I swore…</u>

SPIJAK is drinking steeply. He wavers on his foot.

SPIJAK: … Not this kind of sweat you'll see again. Then will come along this bungalow see – and you remember how the sand never ends as it goes out across the flats, then it's a thin cloudy haze, not blue or white or green to be enough of either, and beyond that – where the waves begin, you can't tell the sea from the sky it is so far – and we're just high enough looking out and squinting our eyes from the verandah. I can't tell you whether it's kids playing far out with a dog or it's a ship's funnel and mast…

Then, he is as he is now in the empty workroom.

SPIJAK: … <u>You never moved that first time, you lay there like stone you were so terrified when I did it to you – held your hands out as far out away from – like a crucifixion…</u> Then, you know, when we get to live by the sea you'll be amazed how long and slow the nights are. And I'm saying to you, Mary, now I won't touch another drop if it kills me not to. And you so fragile…

<u>You were once told it was a miserable pawing act in the dark – a disgusting accident like vomit – to be endured for as little time as possible. The years never changed you. You never did talk about it. And you never remembered to say you loved me. Would you touch me? Not once would you – when my skin cried out for the feather of a finger on it.</u>

The hurt doesn't sober him. He treads water. He shakes his head.

<u>… You could have – once out of a thousand night turned to me and whispered it was something more than the sickness and the evil you believed it. Nights long and arid. Desert not sand. And cold. And I thought it love.</u>

He lowers his hands from his work.

SPIJAK pauses. He lifts up a pile of neatly laid out side seams and forearm seams. He takes them over to the machine. He switches on the little lamp above the bobbin. He lays the first seam under the foot. He starts to run it through. His feet rotate the pedals. He stops mid-seam. He pulls the cloth out from under the foot. He snaps the twin cottons in his teeth. His eyes ache with tears he cannot concede. He picks up all the pieces from the floor beside him and throws them fiercely across his bench at the empty stool of SYDIE's.

The lights lower.

ACT THREE

Early in the morning, first day of January, 1955. The fluorescent lights are out. There are steps outside down to the front door. IRIS enters, in her hat and coat. She switches on the light above ERIC's bench

Lying on the nod-step, wrapped for warmth in cloth rolls, is SPIJAK. The rolley is filled with finished off jackets. All labelled and pressed. SPIJAK's eyes are closed.

She takes out of her bag a box, wrapped in gift paper, which she puts over SPIJAK's head on his bench. She puts another gift box on ERIC's bench, another on MAURICE's bench and she fills the kettles on the side tray, and pours tea into her tea-pot. As she sits down she rubs her hands together –

IRIS: … Cold as a witch's tit…it is.

SPIJAK doesn't stir.

(Reaching for work.) … Tea's up if Eric remembers bring the milk…

She puts her head down over her work.

… God and Mighty it's freezing in here – I've put your New Year pressie on top of the bench – I don't know how you stuck it out – if I'd have known I would have warned you – bosses turn the heating off over Christmas.

She looks up at the suite on the rolley.

IRIS: … You Jews are all the same – too tooting mean for Christmas pressies, New Year they say, that's different they say. Only pressie seen you fork out ever great socking charlie piece of baste work…that's true init – ?

She takes the work across to the machine and runs it under the foot. She pauses –

… 'Course you know, Sydie rang up my landlady Boxing day. She called me to the phone. You ain't seen him have you says Sydie. No I ain't. The silly fucker stitching all

73

holiday says Sydie. If that's what he wants – you know Spijak, Sydie – if that's what, leave him be. Fetch that boy friend around of your'n – fetch out the port and mince pies and put your feet up. But Iris I'm worried. 'Course you are – just exactly what he wants you to be. You like her to feel guilty don't you – ?

She takes work back to the bench.

I know you my lad – you'd have us all feel guilty for want of better craft –

Steps come down to the outside door. MAURICE walks in muffled and wrapped. He jumps about on the floor waving his arms to warm up.

MAURICE: … Morning, Iris.

IRIS: Happy New Year.

MAURICE: *(Jumping about.)* Cold as a witch's fart init – ?

IRIS: Coarse boy you are.

MAURICE: Back seat of the bus – always sit there from Brixton Town Hall – guess what? Some Yuletide yock smashed all the glass out. The draught!

IRIS: Nice Christmas – ?

MAURICE: Played pontoon and did me writing on me play, didn't I – ?

IRIS: Give your Mother something – ?

MAURICE: Give her a book.

IRIS: Lady of leisure she must be – got time to read books.

MAURICE: Masterpiece, it was. I read it before I gave her it.

IRIS: You and your boss just about the same – everything's a masterpiece – suit's a masterpiece, now it's books what are master-pieces. I've never heard you call a kipper a masterpiece.

MAURICE: *The Cruel Sea* by Nicholas Monsarrat. What a book!

IRIS: Did you bring the milk with you I don't think – ?

MAURICE: On twenty-eight bob a week I couldn't afford to bring a milktop.

IRIS: Make you both tea in a minute.

MAURICE stops jumping and waving his arms. As he takes off his thick scarf and his overcoat, he glances under SPIJAK's bench.

MAURICE: Hello!.. it's the greatest tailor of them all!...
How'd he get like that – it's not lunchtime yet...

IRIS: You should either be proud of him –

MAURICE: He hasn't been here all through Christmas has he – ?

IRIS: Or tell him he's a silly fool.

MAURICE: He has!

IRIS: I spoke to Sydie on the phone –

MAURICE: Blimey.

IRIS: She hadn't seen him – so she reckoned –

MAURICE: And I said to myself in the bus – he's going to give us his bleeding-tyrant-business all this week at the top of his voice until that stuff was done.

IRIS: See for yourself.

MAURICE turns towards the rolley, to notice it for the first time, he walks over to the finished jackets.

He ain't going to do much shouting this week, lad.

MAURICE holds one or two finished jackets.

MAURICE: ... He must have sewed his fingers off...

IRIS: That's right.

MAURICE: ... He's done ten finishers in eight days. Look at them.

IRIS: He's a fool.

MAURICE: He couldn't have slept –

IRIS: I've known him work until four in the morning – in the old days when he had Mary –

MAURICE: And he always lay down in the afternoons. Half a bottle of gin and he'd lie down like a baby.

As the kettle begins to whistle, ERIC's steps come down from the road, and he walks in clapping his hands and stamping his feet for the cold.

ERIC: ... Morning morning.

Stamping and bouncing about for the cold.

IRIS: *(To MAURICE.)* I've known Spijak keep himself and Mary at the bench until midnight for a week on end.

ERIC jumps about the room to get warm until he notices SPIJAK.

ERIC: There you are, you old monster! I reckon he's had a good Christmas. Where's he put the empties?

ERIC walks past the rolley taking his hat and coat off. Beneath his coat he has a long inner waistcoat which he unbuttons as well. He steps by the rolley.

ERIC: ... Gawd!...

MAURICE: All his own work, Eric.

ERIC: Gawd!... What a mug!

IRIS: Shame...

MAURICE: Take more'n a skiffle panic to see you do that wouldn't it Eric – ?

ERIC: He needs examining.

ERIC pulls a bottle of milk out of his pocket. He hands it to IRIS who takes it over to the tea tray.

Hot cup of tea, girl, no messing now…

ERIC rolls up his sleeves. MAURICE begins lifting the jackets off the rolley and folding them flat on the bench.

ERIC starts looking about the bench for material. MAURICE has left two jackets on the rolley.

ERIC: There's something missing…

IRIS: *(At the tea tray.)* I always know where everything is –
if there's one thing I am I'm tidy –

ERIC: That blue serge film star job and that cheviot – the
Robert Taylors –

MAURICE: You've done finish on them, you nelly. On the
rolley.

ERIC turns on the two jackets on the rolley, he lifts one off.

Been boozing your Christmas away so much you can't
remember last week.

ERIC: *(Looking at the label.)* I never worked finish on them.
This isn't my work. It's that old Satan's

MAURICE looks around.

ERIC: Look at this, Iris. What a liberty! He's done two of ours.

IRIS: Shame.

ERIC: He must have gone berserk.

MAURICE: Blimey Eric, thank him.

ERIC: You know the rule – it's an unwritten rule you never
touch –

MAURICE: Perhaps he was being nice. Perhaps he meant to do
it – your Christmas present like –

ERIC: What a nerve he's got!

He slaps the jackets down on the bench.

MAURICE: There's not one machine stitch in any of them – bar the back seams and the forearms. Not one. Are yours the same?

ERIC: How could he do this to me – ?

MAURICE: Well are they –?

ERIC looks at the side seams and the sleeves. He nods.

ERIC: I send these up to the front shop – they see I been hand stitching side seams and sleeves they'll cut me jobs down. They'll think I'm doing a Spijak on them.

MAURICE: Go on Eric, give us a smile – he knew you was in skiffle trouble over all these film star jobs – even you with all your machine rubbish – he was trying to help –

ERIC: He knows I wouldn't piss on him if he was on fire –

IRIS: Shame.

ERIC: *(To SPIJAK.)* Allright – I didn't mean it –

ERIC smiles.

MAURICE: Good on you, mate.

ERIC: But I'll run his fingers under the machine I will when he wakes.

MAURICE takes out large sheets of paper. He wraps the paper once round each jacket and neatly pins it. He puts them back one by one on the rolley.

MAURICE: Smile you bugger.

ERIC: Are you asking?

MAURICE: I'm asking.

ERIC: I'm smiling

ERIC grits his teeth in a reluctant smile.

MAURICE: When an old man like that gives you a Christmas present like that – so you should.

ERIC: But I ask myself what does he want from me – for to do such a thing.

MAURICE: Ever heard of gifts, Eric? They're for free.

ERIC: What's free about a gift? There never has been a gift gifted yet what hasn't got a please remit back label on it.

IRIS takes him his cup of tea. Plonks it down in front of him.

IRIS: Mean old sod.

ERIC: How dare you.

IRIS: And that's for free, too.

She glares at him. He lowers his head reluctantly and pins brown paper on the two jackets on the bench which are finished.

IRIS fetches another cup from the tray for MAURICE. He nods. She takes a third cup and puts it by SPIJAK's head.

It's your tea, you tyrant.

He doesn't move.

(Loud.) Right beside your head it is.

He is very still.

Cuchee cuchee… Spijak.

Tickling his ear. But SPIJAK stays still. IRIS puts her hands on the rolls which cover SPIJAK, she tries to encourage him to wake by unravelling them a little.

Come along – it's first of January 1955. Spijak, and the front shop's just caught on fire with all your baste jobs inside.

ERIC: *(To MAURICE.)* Well lad – how's that suit of your'n you're carving up – ?

MAURICE: Collar to be tuck-felled and Sydie'll button-hole it.

ERIC: Nigh enough done.

MAURICE: Finish-press, mate, and that's it.

ERIC: News Chronicle headlines – tailor's boy invents the suit.

IRIS puts her hand from SPIJAK's arm to his forehead. She hastily takes it away.

She stands up, she stares at SPIJAK's face, and she holds out the hand she placed on his forehead.

IRIS: … For God's sake Eric – stop it!

ERIC: Stop what – ?

IRIS: Look at him – he's dead!

MAURICE turns beneath the bench, and tries to pull at SPIJAK. He won't move. He takes all the cloth rolls away from SPIJAK, he pulls at the old man, until he can got a hand underneath SPIJAK. As he tries to lift and pull him out, the weight of SPIJAK's dead body stiffly rolls over onto the floor. The nod-step is a bare nine inches from the floor.

MAURICE looks up at ERIC.

MAURICE: *(Quiet and clear.)* … Eric!

ERIC takes a stop, he kneels beside SPIJAK. He pushes IRIS towards his bench.

ERIC: Sit over there – for Christ's sake!

He touches SPIJAK's face. Both he and MAURICE slowly stand.

IRIS sits on her chair. She closes her eyes tightly.

(In panic, to IRIS.) Just sit there – and don't start screaming and don't start screaming – for Christ's sake will you!

IRIS sits with her eyes tightly closed.

(Quite hysterical.) Just sit there, Iris!

All three of them are frozen into immobility.

There are steps from outside. The door opens, SYDIE walks in. She is well wrapped up, a fur cap and boots. Neither MAURICE, ERIC nor IRIS move an inch. From where SYDIE stands she cannot see SPIJAK on the floor on the far side of the bench.

SYDIE: I was late because after I stepped in D'Arblay Street to order horsehair – so cold it is out – then I was standing outside the shop on the pavement, and who should walk by – but Mickey. You remember Mickey, Iris –

She is taking her cap and her gloves off and reaching to unbutton her coat.

Young Mickey who went to Malaya before Maurice was here – grown a moustache and about four inches taller – so we had a cup of coffee together. He said he's working with a Vicuna import company – sales ledgers and that – packed the trade up altogether. Says there's more money in filling up an accounts' book with figures than there is in craft. All those years teaching Mickey the trade – right up the spout.

She stands there looking at them. They don't move.

SYDIE: *(Cont.)* ... Happy New Year, all.

The lights lower.

It is a few days later. As the lights lift, the room is empty. SPIJAK's bench has been completely tidied up. There are a number of suits hanging on the rolley.

On the steps outside come down ERIC and IRIS. They enter. They are wearing black for mourning. ERIC has a handsome bowler. IRIS carefully takes off her gloves.

IRIS: ... Fancy.

ERIC: What is – ?

IRIS: Shame on that Rabbi.

ERIC: What did he do, Iris – ask you for a contribution – ?

IRIS: He said to Sydie – when we come out he said – do you
wish to keep the ashes at home or shall I put the vase in
the wall beside Mary – ?

ERIC: Well you got to know that sort of thing ain't you. Can't
just leave Spijak's ashes in Kensal Rise like that can you.
Next week they'll have him as a door-step.

IRIS: Can't just give a service – and everyone's in a state of
shock – and suddenly ask Sydie if she wants the ashes back.

ERIC: I remember an old kipper – her maker hit the bench –
and she kept the ashes on the front mantelpiece.

IRIS: Shame.

ERIC: Alabaster vase – posy of roses round it and carved with
his initials, right on the top of the Aga cosy stove.

IRIS: Where's your reverence.

ERIC: I'll say one thing – it'll be a lot quieter in Dover Street
without him.

IRIS: He loved to shout.

ERIC: Loved it.

IRIS: If anybody ever asks me what I remember most about
him – I'd say his shouting.

ERIC: That's right.

> *They have taken their coats off, and they settle down at the bench.*
> *IRIS wears her apron. ERIC rolls up his sleeves.*

… Ain't you going to the lavatory, Iris – ?

IRIS: No.

ERIC: But you always go to the lavatory before you start in the
morning –

IRIS: Just don't feel the urge thank you.

ERIC: You been standing in the rain for an hour at the cemetery – you must want to.

IRIS: Besides – it's your turn to buy the loo paper – blinking disgrace us girls having to go in there – you so mean.

ERIC: Put your head down and keep your fingers felling up that stay tape.

Down the outside stairs come MAURICE and SYDIE. They enter. SYDIE is in black, a rather shiny black suit fitted very tightly, and her high heels. MAURICE is wearing his own finished suit, a white shirt and a black tie.

IRIS: … Morning.

SYDIE: Morning, Iris.

MAURICE: Morning, Eric.

ERIC doesn't look up from his work. SYDIE takes off her topcoat and reaches for her apron. MAURICE rolls up his sleeves.

ERIC: *(To MAURICE.)* … I had to park the car first – so when I stood in the chapel at the back – I said to myself that's a fair old collar and shoulders up in the front by the Rabbi. I didn't recognise you Maurice.

MAURICE very carefully hangs his jacket on the rolley.

Fair enough that suit is, lad.

MAURICE: Thanks.

ERIC: Very fair indeed. Press it yourself – ?

MAURICE: I didn't send it to the cleaners did I – ?

ERIC: Best suit I ever saw a boy make – turn around –

MAURICE reluctantly shows ERIC the trousers and the waistcoat.

Best making up I ever did see – for a boy –

MAURICE: Not so much of the boy.

ERIC lifts the jackets up from the rolley.

ERIC: And look at this Iris – not a machine stitch nowhere – but for the backseam – not one. It's perfect. And it's perfect colour too ain't it?

MAURICE: What do you mean – colour?

ERIC: Perfect colour for – no disrespect mind you not trying it on – it's just made for a funeral init?

IRIS: Shame.

ERIC: Straight up –

IRIS: That's not nice, that's all.

ERIC: He looked a prince in that suit, I'm trying to say.

MAURICE and SYDIE exchange pieces of work. ERIC goes back to his bench.

SYDIE: … I don't think that's coming out right…

MAURICE: Lunchtime I'll get new needles – we need seven and eight sharps and we need five and six betweens –

SYDIE: That horsehair ain't arrived neither –

MAURICE: I'll chase them. If you find me the bill I'll take it in to the front shop.

They put their heads down to the work.

ERIC: … Give it the gun, Iris, then.

She looks up at him and wipes her eyes.

IRIS: I can't.

ERIC: We've missed half the morning –

IRIS: You just don't understand…

She is sniffing with tears. And she tries to wipe her eyes with the cloth she is working.

IRIS: You ain't got no heart…

ERIC: Do a bit of work – you'll feel better.

IRIS: *(Real tears.)* I wanted to tell you what I done.

ERIC: *(Softly but impatiently.)* Tell it then…

IRIS: I went and bought two tickets.

ERIC: What did you went and bought two tickets about – ?

IRIS: You know how you always say you love the opera –
I went to the booking agency and I bought two tickets.
For me and you.

ERIC: Now don't drop tears all over that flap pocket –

IRIS: Called Cavalleria Rusticana and Pagliacci. One for you
and one for me – so's we could go together.

ERIC: That's very kind of you dear, but –

IRIS: You always did say you liked the opera – and you're such
a mean rotten maker to me you'd never think I might like
to see a nice night out –

ERIC: I'm trying to thank you aren't I –

IRIS has burst into a flood of tears.

IRIS: You're so mean – you're a scrooging skimping bachelor
you are – and I been your kipper for since the war ended
and when have you ever been kind to me?

ERIC: *(With feeling.)* Don't be like that.

IRIS: I'm bloody crying Eric –

ERIC: All right all right –

IRIS: Crying me eyes out and you just don't understand do
you…!

ERIC: Iris, please!

He starts to sniff and wipe his eyes. He has to put down his work.

IRIS: So mean you have been –

ERIC: Now you're making me cry –

IRIS: So you should –

ERIC: *(Crying now properly.)* I can't see what I'm doing.

IRIS: About time.

They both stand and reach for a large length of cotton and both wipe their eyes together.

They resume their seats. ERIC perched on his bench.

IRIS: So are you coming with me – to see this Pagliacci thing – ?

ERIC: Course I'm coming.

IRIS: I know you've always said how much you appreciate cultural things and that like – isn't that true – and they cost one pound five each the tickets.

ERIC: I did I did.

The emphasis on the stage crosses to the other side, where MAURICE and SYDIE work. ERIC and IRIS put their heads down.

MAURICE: … Smile, Sydie.

SYDIE: *(Definitely not.)* I'm smiling.

MAURICE: I'll see you home tonight.

SYDIE: I'm working

MAURICE: I'll take the train with you.

SYDIE: I'll be fine.

MAURICE: Take it easy in the mornings – there ain't much to do – come in at ten.

SYDIE: No thanks.

The phone starts to ring. ERIC rushes ever to it.

ERIC: *(Into the mouthpiece.)* ... Eric here. Who? ...
You don't want to speak to me!... I see.

He holds the phone out towards MAURICE. ERIC looks ver surprised.

... It's for you.

MAURICE takes the phone.

MAURICE: ... Hallo.

ERIC returns to the bench.

ERIC: *(To IRIS.)* ... First time the guv'nor's ever said he don't
want to talk to me that is.

MAURICE: *(Into the mouthpiece.)* Yes...

*SYDIE takes her handbag and walks to the side door to the step up
to the lavatory.*

IRIS: *(Looks up at SYDIE.)* You'll need some paper Sydie...

*SYDIE closes the door behind her. She reaches the washing and runs
the tap. She washes her hands and her face. Whatever tears she has in
her eyes she dowses away with the water. The light lifts in the toilet.*

MAURICE: *(Listening to the voice on the phone.)* ... Yes, sir...
completely...that's right...

*SYDIE glances through the open door of the lavatory. The floor is
covered with torn up bits of manuscript paper. She kneels to look at
them. They are all neatly torn into square fragments. Hundreds of
them. They slip through her fingers and glide across the tiles.*

*MAURICE put the phone back. He looks rather proud and yet sad.
ERIC watches him. MAURICE walks over to the contract for his
apprenticeship which is pinned on the wall where SPIJAK first placed
it. He takes it down and tears it up with his hands.*

ERIC: ... What did he say to you – ?

MAURICE: Never you mind.

ERIC: My business, Eric.

ERIC: Don't tell me – the guv'nor's given you your cards…
am I right?

MAURICE doesn't reply. He climbs back on his bench. He picks up his work.

SYDIE comes back upstairs. She closes the side door behind her.

IRIS: *(Glancing up.)* … There – didn't I say – no paper down
there at all – shameful init…

SYDIE: *(A beat: then –)* …it's all right, Iris. It's all right now.
There's plenty of paper down there.

She walks past MAURICE. She stops to stare at him.

… Maurice – ?

MAURICE: *(Head down.)* Hallo…

SYDIE: You…a bloody fool…you just an idiot you know. You
was free…the door is open. Nobody could stop you. Eric
ain't going to shout if you did a Mickey on us. There's
nothing for to stay for, boy… Nobody wanted my Father's
craft so don't think on account of me that – …

Her voice trails. He keeps on sewing. She stares at him. He will not look, she takes her place behind the bench.

The RUNNER's feet come down the outside stairs. The door is kicked open. One by one the bundles start flying through the air. ERIC leaps about to catch them.

RUNNER'S VOICE: … Eric!

Then another.

… Eric!

Another bundle.

… Eric!

ERIC stands there with his hands held out for more. There is a pause.

RUNNER'S VOICE: ... And – Maurice!

A bundle wings through the air at MAURICE's head. ERIC looks amazed.

ERIC: Maurice!

RUNNER'S VOICE: ... And – Maurice!

MAURICE catches the second bundle. SYDIE is staring up at him, her eyes wide.

The RUNNER shuts the door and his feet pound up the steps.

ERIC: What in hell's going on!

SYDIE watches MAURICE take the two bundles and places them on SPIJAK's empty bench. MAURICE quickly unwraps the bundles SYDIE stands and stares. IRIS puts her work down and watches too.

MAURICE: One baste blue herringbone for Friday.

SYDIE: One what – ?

MAURICE: One baste and half finish tweed for a single fitting Tuesday week.

MAURICE holds up the notes attached to each bundle and quickly seams them.

SYDIE: But –

MAURICE: There's a right sleeve one inch short – one left neck shrink in – button-hole twice on turnbacks – side vents dummy pleat what mustn't show when open. Right – ?

SYDIE: Right.

MAURICE: On the doublebreasted there's a three quarter length roll – you sew both buttons but the top button has to roll with the canvas.

SYDIE: *(Beginning to smile.)* Understood.

MAURICE: It's all night till nine o'clock tonight and tomorrow night – and it's eight o'clock Saturday morning to this lot away.

SYDIE: What about –

MAURICE: Never you mind what about – first thing I mean you make sure that horsehair comes in –

SYDIE: Wait a minute –

MAURICE: And new packet needles as well – keep the bill I'll need it –

SYDIE: But Maurice –

MAURICE: Put your head down, girl.

End.

By the same author

Lee Harvey Oswald
A Far Mean Streak of Independence Brought on by Negleck
9781783190775

Tom and Viv
9781840026801

Calico
9781840024050

WWW.OBERONBOOKS.COM

Follow us on www.twitter.com/@oberonbooks
& www.facebook.com/OberonBooksLondon

www.ingramcontent.com/pod-product-compliance
Ingram Content Group UK Ltd.
Pitfield, Milton Keynes, MK11 3LW, UK
UKHW020706060325
455689UK00012B/122